Boxer's Book of Conditioning & Drilling
Mark Hatmaker

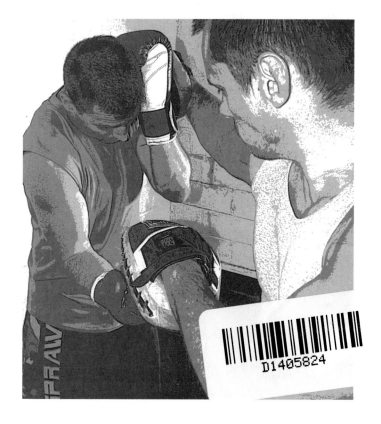

Cover photo by Mitch Thomas
Interior photos by Doug Werner

TRACKS

Tracks Publishing
San Diego, California

Boxer's Book of Conditioning & Drilling
Mark Hatmaker

Tracks Publishing
140 Brightwood Avenue
Chula Vista, CA 91910
619-476-7125
tracks@cox.net
www.startupsports.com
trackspublishing.com

Copyright © 2011 by Doug Werner and Mark Hatmaker
10 9 8 7 6 5 4 3 2 1

Publisher's Cataloging-in-Publication

Hatmaker, Mark.

   Boxer's book of conditioning & drilling / Mark Hatmaker ; cover photo by Mitch Thomas ; interior photos by Doug Werner. -- San Diego, Calif. : Tracks Pub., c2011.

     p. ; cm.
     ISBN: 978-1-935937-28-9
     Includes index.

     1. Boxing--Training. 2. Boxers (Sports)--Training.
3. Plyometrics. 4. Physical education and training. I. Werner, Doug, 1950- II. Title.

GV1137.6 .H383 2011   2011935612
796.83--dc23   1110

Books by Mark Hatmaker

No Holds Barred Fighting:
The Ultimate Guide to Submission Wrestling

More No Holds Barred Fighting:
Killer Submissions

No Holds Barred Fighting:
Savage Strikes

No Holds Barred Fighting:
Takedowns

No Holds Barred Fighting:
The Clinch

No Holds Barred Fighting:
The Ultimate Guide to Conditioning

No Holds Barred Fighting:
The Kicking Bible

No Holds Barred Fighting:
The Book of Essential Submissions

Boxing Mastery

No Second Chance:
A Reality-Based Guide to Self-Defense

MMA Mastery:
Flow Chain Drilling and Integrated O/D Training

MMA Mastery:
Ground and Pound

MMA Mastery:
Strike Combinations

Boxer's Book of Conditioning & Drilling

Books are available through major bookstores
and booksellers on the Internet.

Dedicated to all the "Sweet Scientists" out there who have experimented and continue to experiment in the gyms and rings of the world pushing the sport and science ever further.

Acknowledgments
Phyllis Carter
Kylie Hatmaker
Dan Marx
Mitch Thomas

Contents

Warning label
The fighting arts include contact and can be dangerous. Use proper equipment and train safely. Practice with restraint and respect for your partners. Drill for fun, fitness and to improve skills. Do not fight with the intent to do harm.

"Fights are won in the gym, not in the ring."

— Unknown

Stop me if you've heard this one before. Nah, scratch that, I'm going to say it anyway. I'm going to hit you with something you've heard time and again, something you already know. Something you've heard come out of the mouths of boxing coaches, trainers and ringside commentators hundreds (if not thousands) of times. And we can only assume that this bit of repeated advice was being uttered in some form or another long before someone decided to write it down. You ready for repetition #4,347,771?

"Fights are won in the gym, not in the ring."

Too bad we can't track down with any surety who first uttered these wise words so we could give them full credit, but my guess is that some form of this advice has been around as long as human beings decided to make a sport out of smacking each other around. We can easily imagine pancratium masters in ancient Greece exhorting their protégés with these wise words, or gladiator trainers (doctores) urging their charges on with some version of the phrase.

"Chance favors only the prepared mind."

— Dr. Louis Pasteur

This advice holds true not only in boxing but in all combat sports. Wrestling has a long tradition of brutal training regimens, and today's mixed martial arts (MMA) fighters have adopted the axiom as well. In truth, the axiom holds for all human endeavors that require any level of elevated performance. Whether it be competitive sprinting, heightened musicianship, chess prowess, military endeavors, you name it — if it requires a level of skill, the key to successful performance lies in the training — not the mere observation of the end result. In other words, to paraphrase the axiom, what we see in the ring is indicative of what preceded it in the gym/training phase. Or performance is a reflection of the work that preceded it. If you don't like what you see reflected, you know how to change it.

I repeat, performance level in the ring or any endeavor is more a reflection of preparation than that of any other variable. Yes, luck does factor in, no doubt about that. We have to accept the phenomenon of the lucky punch, the "out of nowhere" dropper, but we can draw some comfort from a corollary to "Fights are won in the gym, not in the ring." That corollary is the axiom "Chance favors the prepared mind." (We can source this one — Dr. Louis Pasteur.)

Let's be precise and respectful of Dr. Pasteur and give the more literal translation of his quote. What he actually said was, "In the fields of observation, chance favors only the prepared mind." The literal translation is a bit narrower, but to our advantage because it more readily highlights the wisdom of the first axiom. The nice, more loosely translated version of Dr. Pasteur's quote leads one to think that preparation is ideal, but apparently chance also favors random individuals in an infinite number of scenarios. In other words, if we were allowed to put 100 professionally trained boxers in the ring with the best version of Mike Tyson, we can imagine or expect a sizable proportion of those professionally trained 100 to do rather well. But the loose version of the quote also allows for the possibility that out of 100 nontrained folks entering the ring *mano a mano* with Iron Mike, a handful might do well via chance alone.

Now, honestly, can you picture any of the average Joes you meet on a day-to-day basis coming out on top in a head-to-head match with the 21-year-old Iron Mike? I can't. Let's return to the strict interpretation of the esteemed doctor's quote, "Chance favors only the prepared mind." The word "only" is key. Your "luck" is wholly and solely dependent on your level of preparation.

OK, I've restated an obvious training axiom and belabored the loose translation of the words of a dead French scientist. To what purpose you may ask? There is a tendency to focus on the end result of training — the glory of victory, the appreciation of smooth performance. But what we see in the ring, the end result, is but the tip of the iceberg.

I want to take away all wiggle room regarding getting your butt into the gym. I want to kill any excuse generating mechanism that allows anyone not to do what must be done to be a successful boxer (successful anything for that matter). I want to remove any and all barriers between you and luck. As we know, luck, by definition, is a chance thing. If you are so lucky as to have some once-in-a-lifetime chance in your favor, and you see it and recognize it for what it is, but you didn't do the prep work to capitalize, well, then, you have no one to blame but yourself. So say again ...

"Fights are won in the gym, not in the ring."

10,000 hours[1]

10,000 hours? What's that? That is the consensus estimate of how many hours of training it takes to master a subject or skill. Ten thousand hours is a lot of time. We have 8,760 hours available to us per year. Out of those 8,760 hours, we have to find time to eat, sleep, earn a living, relax with friends and family and a few other necessities. Where are we going to find these 10,000 hours?

Let's assume an industry standard of eight hours per night sleeping for a total of 2,920 hours. That leaves only 5,840 of our yearly total. Let's add in a day job and assume full-time hours with weekends off, a couple of weeks for vacation and a few personal days scattered

---

1. For books on the 10,000 hours hypotheses see *The Genius in All of Us* by David Shenk or *Talent is Overrated* by Geoff Colvin. If you've got time for only one, go with Shenk.

10,000 hours? What's that? That is the consensus estimate of how many hours of training it takes to master a subject or skill. here and there. That uses up an estimated 1,920 hours per year leaving us 3,929 hours. We still have to eat, commute to and from work, go to the store, shower, hit the bathroom, interact with friends and family, veg in front of the TV, Xbox or the Net (insert needless vice of your choosing here). Figure your own numbers to subtract. So where are these 10,000 hours going to come from?

Before we try to find the time, let's first recognize that the 10,000 hours number refers to mastery or elite level performance. It does not refer to competent performance, "pretty damn good" performance or great performance. Ten thousand hours merely gives us a rough ETA for the apex of performance. That means somewhere between zero hours and 10,000 hours there is an entire spectrum of skill that we can attain and use to our benefit along the way. Giving up at zero because one can't jump to 10,000 is ludicrous. There are many excellent athletes not at the 10,000-hour mark who make good use of their current in between measures. The key is to not see the 10,000 hours number as a barrier, but as an impetus — a metaphorical fire under the posterior to get to work now recognizing that even the first hour of training contributes to

The way to 10,000 hours begins right now — at minute one.

the 10,000 hour total. On the other hand, procrastination (choosing defeat by default) gets you nothing.

How about another quote? This one is from either Lao Tzu or Confucius depending on your source.

"The journey of a thousand miles begins with a single step."

Let's paraphrase this to better fit our needs:

The way to 10,000 hours begins right now — at minute one.

Are you experienced?

Mr. Hendrix asked this very question referring to an area of endeavor outside the focus of this book, but the question is still pertinent. The aforementioned 10,000 hour mark leads many to believe that simply putting in the time makes us golden, but, alas, not so much.
If time were simply all it took to be great, we'd have to come up with a new word for great because great would be the new average. To illustrate how experience and longevity aren't all they are cracked up to be, look at those around you. Those who have been in

their jobs for lengthy periods, those who have been weekend athletes or after work gym rats for years. To be blunt, look to your own personal lives. Look at how many years you have been a husband, a wife, a father, a mother, a son, a daughter, a friend. Ask yourself if experience and years on the job are all it takes. Are you the best husband, wife, father, mother, son, daughter, friend, employee, employer or weekend athlete you can be? Does your current performance match your years of experience?

Before anyone gets insulted, we all have areas where we have "years on the job" and yet perform like rookies. You've probably heard this key question before, "Do you have five years experience or have you repeated the same year five times?" That two-pronged question is what designing better training regimens is about — not repeating the same year again and again but always progressing. This breaking of stalemate work and commitment to continuous progression is called, in cognitive learning circles, deliberate practice.

Deliberate practice spells all the difference. Let's be honest, most of us are athletes who put random time in the gym lifting some weights here, banging the bag there and overall simply maintaining what skill and conditioning levels we had when we walked through the door. Utilizing deliberate practice, this very same athlete could potentially spend as much time in the gym (in many cases even less) with progressively designed General Physical Preparedness (GPP) and Specific Physical Preparedness (SPP) training regimens and always edge onward and upward (more on these two later).

Deliberate practice requires that we always keep an eye on weaknesses whether these be in conditioning (quickly fatiguing shoulders, poor recovery between rounds and the like), or in specific skill work (such as poor elbow alignment in hooks or lagging footwork), and address our weaknesses, whatever they may be at the time, and bring them up to snuff. Deliberate practice asks us to continuously monitor all aspects of our game (conditioning and skill) and always tweak components of our training to inch our conditioning and skill work ever upward.

The deliberate practice approach to training says that we cannot simply put in hours at the gym with our minds disengaged. We must be ever aware of what we are doing at the very moment we are doing it while also keeping an eye on where we want to be. We must assess daily and ask the question, "What can I do today, do right now that will lend itself to closing the gap between my present ability and my ideal self?"

With this working definition of deliberate practice in mind, ask yourself, right now this minute, whether what you're doing in the gym is moving you forward and adding to your experience, or are you spinning your wheels repeating year one.

Deliberate practice asks us to continuously monitor all aspects of our game (conditioning and skill) and always tweak components of our training to inch our conditioning and skill work ever upward.

Marginal Revolution

Pop Quiz:

1. What's the difference between 9.89 seconds and 9.69 seconds?

2. What's the difference between 7 feet 8 inches and 7 feet 8.8 inches?

Answer to both:
The difference is earning a Gold Medal or a Silver Medal in the Olympics.

Richard Thompson is a world-class Olympic athlete who ran the 100 meters in the 2008 Olympics in 9.89 seconds. He came in second to Usain Bolt, losing by .2 seconds. That .8 inch difference earned Andrey Silnov the Gold in the 2008 high jump over Germaine Mason's Silver.

You'd think .8 inch wouldn't matter? Tell that to Germaine Mason. You'd think .2 seconds, or even the "wide margin" of two seconds in the 200 meter freestyle (Park Tae-Hwan's Silver versus Michael Phelps's Gold) isn't that significant. But it turns out that tiny improvements, improvements at the margins, are often what spell the difference between winning and

But it turns out that tiny improvements, improvements at the margins, are often what spell the difference between winning and losing at the elite level.

losing at the elite level. These silver medalists are astonishing world-class athletes who have nothing to be ashamed of, but did you know their names? You probably know the names of the men they lost to, Usain Bolt and Michael Phelps (maybe not Andrey Silnov unless you are a high jump enthusiast).

Look at those margins again. The differences between victory and recognition and second place anonymity at the high end of any sport are s-n-u-g. These tight, tight differences between winning and losing need to be addressed. For that we borrow the phrase "marginal revolution," a term coined by economists Tyler Cowen and Alexander Tabarrok. This esteemed duo defines marginal revolution as the tiny changes/tweaks that can be made to a system that result in large changes at the end point (Gold versus Silver, for example). These tiny tweaks, these marginal improvements are what steadily accrue into large rewards.

To illustrate this point in monetary terms, the way to wealth isn't flailing about looking for the big payoff (the lottery win, the lucky stock pick, to be "discovered") but socking away earnings into an account that accumulates compound interest (good luck in today's economy). The person looking for the "Big Win" we'll call the Gambler, and the saver/investor we'll call the Marginal Revolutionary. We can also refer to those who dabble as Wheel Spinners — those who mean well but never quite get the discipline engine in gear.

The Gambler drifts from get-rich-quick scheme to get-rich-quick scheme, this "foolproof" investment to that "foolproof" investment, this business start-up plan or that one I heard about on the Internet, and so on. The Gambler has all his eggs in one basket. The Marginal Revolutionary, on the other hand, is always on the move making small but steady incremental progress. Seeking tiny upticks in income and socking that away into interest bearing investments. Note the Gambler's strategy may or may not work (probably not), but the Marginal Revolutionary is seeing some form of success with each monthly statement.

The Marginal Revolutionary is distinguished from the Wheel Spinner investor as well. The Wheel Spinner saves money sometimes, sometimes not. He keeps a budget, but often exceeds it, which eats away at the incremental work of the investment. In other words, he repeats year one's investment strategy again and again while never actually progressing — never recognizing the wisdom of the Marginal Revolutionary who allows the incremental improvements to add up creating million dollar incomes with diligent work.

Let's bring this back to sport. Are you the Spinning Wheel Athlete who does the same routine day in, day out at the gym no matter what level of success (or lack of) it brings you? The Wheel Spinner maintains the status quo, he leaves the gym no better than when he walked through the door. Are you the Gambling Athlete who drifts from diet to diet, this hot new training regimen of the week to that training flavor of the month? Do you say "I'll be in the gym every day for three hours" yet see that resolve often trickle to a few visits here or there because you've set the workload or immediate goals too high?

Or are you the Marginal Revolutionary who picks a sure but steady path — the path that emphasizes the fundamentals of both conditioning and technique? The Marginal Revolutionary doesn't strive to reinvent the wheel like the Gambler, or ride on that wheel until the tires are bald like the Wheel Spinner. Are you the Marginal Revolutionary who recognizes that we don't need to reinvent the wheel, but there's nothing wrong with constantly tweaking air pressure here, balance there, get a realignment every so often to make the perfectly functioning wheel a bit more efficient?

It is with marginal daily improvement and being ever aware of not spinning our wheels or being the foolhardy gambler that much of the material contained herein is based. We must recognize that once we gain a fundamental level of skill and conditioning, we must have ways to make small tweaks to nudge our progress upward. The Marginal Revolutionary recognizes that small is just fine. Every increment we gain is always a gain — no matter how small.

Every incre-
ment we gain
is always a
gain — no
matter how
small.

GPP vs. SPP

To find these marginal improvements, we look to the above two sets of initials. Basically, if one is constructing physical training regimens that involve many elements (strength, stamina, speed, explosiveness) there are only two broad ways to attack the subject — GPP or SPP.

First, a definition of the initials.

GPP — General Physical Preparedness

SPP — Specific Physical Preparedness

Second, a brief bit about each approach, and then we'll discuss why it is vital to marry the two.

The GPP approach to training seeks to increase the body's adaptive systems to a variety of potential physical stressors whether they are improved response to load bearing, increased adaptability to long-term endurance work, quick recovery post anaerobic bursts and the like. The GPP approach does not assume specific end tasks (training for this or that specific sport), and this lack of single focus is reflected in the makeup of the GPP program. A GPP program can consist of exercises and regimens from many sports, sports out-

> "Everyone has a plan until they get punched in the face."
> — Mike Tyson

side any specific area of focus to contribute to the whole.

GPP exercise choices can include power lifting, Olympic lifts, bodyweight exercises, basic gymnastics work, sprints (short to mid-distance), rowing, rope climbing, sledge-hammer work, tire-flipping and on and on. In other words, GPP advocates a broad based (general) approach to the goal of improving overall fitness that may be applied to a broad (general) variety of stressors/physical challenges. In short, GPP gives little thought to the end result or what the GPP will be used for. GPP is more concerned with "ifs" or "just in case" scenarios and not certainties.

The SPP approach is seemingly diametrically opposed to GPP in that SPP begins with the end in mind. SPP programs assume that you know exactly what sport/task is being trained for and thus make exercise/regimen selections based solely on contingencies encountered in the specific outcome. These outcomes can be boxing matches, marathons or long-range patrol missions. With the known outcome in mind, the trainer, coach or athlete is able to construct a program that is reflective of what most definitely will be and perhaps give a little bit of thought to "maybes."

A sample SPP program for, let's say boxing (surprise) would stun no one if it included roadwork, heavy bag training, focus pad sessions, some weight training, skipping rope and the like. You may already notice that there is more similarity between GPP and SPP than one would at first imagine. Although in the boxing ring there is no lifting competition, the boxer still trains with weights. Likewise, there is no push-up competition yet he still does push-ups, and although there is no running race, he still runs. SPP may train with a known outcome in mind, but the broad based (general) approach is still utilized.

Beyond the borrowing of a few conditioning methods from other sports, there might be even more of a reason to marry the GPP and SPP approaches. That reason lies in one tiny crack in the logic behind SPP conditioning. The crack is certainty. Yes, sports have set rules and to some degree predictable outcomes (predictable as to how the play will be conducted), but assumptions beyond the limits of rule play may be a bit misplaced. I offer a quote from one of boxing's legends that takes a knock at certainty.

"Everyone has a plan until they get punched in the face." — Mike Tyson

Don't misunderstand me, the uncertainty in a specific sport isn't a worry that you will suddenly be required to pole vault in the middle of round three or that tennis players will suddenly be confronted with a downhill slalom. The certainty of the rules of play is not in question here. We must marry GPP and SPP approaches within reason. What is in question are some assumptions about boundaries of conditioning performance required for a particular sport.

Let's take one aspect of a boxing match, the main aspect, the punch (any punch you choose). Let's hypothesize what fuels that punch and see if we can figure out exactly which approach makes a successful punch what it is — a GPP or an SPP approach.

1. Good Punching Technique — SPP, undoubtedly.

2. Good Footwork to get the puncher there — SPP.

3. Good timing on the punch — Another one for SPP.

4. Good power — Could be heavy bag work (SPP), push-ups (GPP) or bench presses (GPP). Since power comes from the ground up, it could also be roadwork (GPP), rope work (GPP), squats (GPP), plyometric box work (GPP) or core work (GPP).

5. Punching well under duress — SPP sparring work, definitely and perhaps a bit of the resolve forged by tough GPP metabolic sessions.

6. Punching well late in the rounds despite fatigue, showing good adaptation to continuing workload — SPP sure, but we probably also have to tip the hat toward GPP.

7. Punching well off balance — Thank GPP instability work that "woke up" and conditioned muscles seldom used in predictable balance or terrain conditions.

By committing oneself to the **mastery** of the given sport's technical vocabulary and **preparing** oneself for unpredictable but reasonable variables, one can hasten the trip on the road to experience.

You get the idea. We can be certain about the sport itself, its rules and technical approaches, but there may be a bit less certainty how a system as complex as the human body will adapt to the work. Plans have a tendency to experience entropy/change on the fly, and when that happens, we have only two ways to cope with change.

1. Hope our journey to 10,000 hours of mastery (SPP) has progressed enough to deal with the new variables or ...

2. Hope that our varied conditioning (GPP) can buy us a little time to cope/cruise through the uncertainty until a bit of order can be restored.

The first option is easier to control than the second. We can't become time travelers and magically be 3,000 hours further into our 10,000 hour journey. No, we're all subject to the same 60 seconds per minute rate and will eventually get there in time. But we can control coping with strategy number two. While we're building our 10,000-hour bank of experience, we can invest in GPP conditioning insurance and gamble that it will see us through some of the rough spots our hours haven't taken us yet.

The Marginal Revolutionary embraces both SPP and GPP recognizing that whereas sports are closed, somewhat predictable systems, the human body is an open complex system. By committing oneself to the mastery of the given sport's technical vocabulary and preparing oneself for unpredictable but reasonable variables, one can hasten the trip on the road to experience. In other words, utilize both SPP and GPP. SPP is your plan, and GPP is your backup when you get punched in the face.

Optimal mixture

With all this preaching the gospel of mixing GPP and SPP, we must not lose sight of how to mix and in what proportions. Yes, we need to borrow from other sports to build our GPP base, but just how much do we borrow?

For example, we need roadwork, but just how much? Will wind sprints do the job or do I need the ability to run marathons? If I bench press to contribute to punching power, do I need low to moderate weight or do I need to approach competitive power lifting poundages?

The key to optimal mixture is to define your SPP goal. Easy enough here — boxing. Once the SPP goal has been identified, we then enumerate necessary physical attributes. On the next page is a sample list.

Attribute Demands for boxing

1. Good adaptation to prolonged cardiovascular demands. Think the ability to perform well in late rounds.

2. Quick recovery following anaerobic threshold efforts. Think post-flurry recovery or in between rounds returning the cardiovascular system back to a reasonable plateau.

3. Superior muscular stamina in the legs. Think never going flatfooted even in later rounds.

4. Superior muscular stamina in the shoulder girdle, chest, back, triceps and biceps keep your punches popping once you pass fresh rounds.

5. Superior strength in the legs, shoulders, chest, back and arms to put hammer power in your punches.

6. Strong and endurance tested core to unite the upper and lower body for synergized power.

7. Resilient core built to resist repeated impact.

8. Superior response to eccentric cardiovascular demands post-stress/post-impact. It's one thing to have good stamina in your roadwork or bag work, but it's a completely different animal to have stamina when absorbing punishment.

9. Superior fast-twitch response to fire fast shots or to quickly respond defensively.

10. Elite mind toughness to keep on keeping on — doing your job in the face of the plan-changing punches to the face.

It's not necessarily the quantity of work done (years of experience), but the caliber of the work done (deliberate practice).

This is a short list, but it covers what should be the main attributes required of the boxer. Once we have these attributes in mind, we then test all proposed GPP and SPP training ideas and see if they meet the criteria of the Attribute Demands list. If they do not, then you may have something that is for GPP only, something that you can leave out of the mixture allowing you to not waste your time to getting further down the road to 10,000 hours. If it does meet the criteria, well, then you have another tool for the toolbox that will benefit both GPP and SPP.

More is always better, right?

There is a dilemma that faces top performers who are driven to sprint down the 10,000-hour road. That dilemma is the assumption that if x amount of a particular conditioning process is a plus then even more x is better. Turns out this is not always the case.

Take the example of roadwork — running bolsters cardiovascular performance and adds some pep to the legs. Boxing has a long tradition of utilizing roadwork for the above two goals, and running to aid these goals is not in question. What is in question is how much running is necessary and how much is too much.

Let's take a look at an arbitrary boxing roadwork program and assume that the athlete wants to put in five days a week equal to the overall length of his event. Assuming a 10-rounder, that's 35 minutes including rounds and between round times. So we compute a commitment run of approximately one half hour per session.

Another fighter believes roadwork is a key component of training. He reasons that since his opponent is doing 35 minutes per day, he'll reap twice the benefits if he doubles the roadwork. Makes sense in a surface sort of way, doesn't it? As a matter of fact, it would make perfect sense if the athlete were training for long-distance running, but does it makes sense to double the roadwork for boxing preparation?

Today's top exercise physiologists are rediscovering and confirming what was intuitively known by many of the great athletes years ago. It's not necessarily the quantity of work done (years of experience), but the caliber of the work done (deliberate practice). More often than not, conditioning is not about quantity but quality. Not how far or how long you run, but how you run. Not how many push-ups you can do, but the quality of the push-ups you do. There is one area where quantity is given the upper hand. It is in lifting weights. But even here, good quality lifts are vital or you risk injury or missed strength opportunities as you hedge your lifts.

Back to the roadwork conundrum. Why might the doubling of the roadwork be a bad idea? First of all, whatever time you put into your GPP is time spent that cannot be invested in SPP. With that in mind, we must strive to invest only in high-quality, efficient GPP so we can get back on the 10,000-hour road as quickly as possible. Second, the quality of the roadwork as it relates to the needs of boxing might render the hour and ten minutes impossible. I don't mean that it is impossible to run for an hour and ten minutes, people do it every day. What I am saying is that the variety of running most conducive to boxing training is impossible to sustain over such a long time interval.

Boxing requires rapid expenditures of high energy with periodic moments of reduced work rate recovery. It would be ideal if our roadwork reflected those circumstances. In other words, rather than setting the clock for 35 minutes or 70 minutes, it might be wiser to alter roadwork to a series of wind sprints (to emulate the flurries) interspersed with jogging (or even rest periods) to train the system to find recovery on the move. If an athlete finds that he can do this sort of intense work for 35 minutes straight (let alone 70), I wager that he simply isn't sprinting hard enough. Paradoxically, proper quality/intensity ensures more (better) work in less time.

Another less obvious minus to the "the more roadwork the better" approach is the loss of snap or pep in the legs. Without getting into all the fun biophysical jargon, long-distance running trains slow-twitch muscle fibers. The more we train/recruit slow-twitch muscle fiber the less we call on fast-twitch muscle fiber. As a result, those who consistently train long-distance running show poor performance in vertical jumps (even if they had previously shown good jump performance). For boxers, this translates to more running equals less snap in the legs.

It is with an eye on both the obvious and less obvious aspects of any GPP and SPP approach that we must design our training. As a rule, let the training choices be reflective of the Attribute Demands list, emphasize intensity levels reflective of the sports work-rate curve, all the while making sure that your mixture is not fostering gains in one area while diminishing attributes in another, thus hamstringing your progress.

Tradition versus innovation

Do the activities on the following list look like good ideas to improve your boxing?

1. Afternoon horseback riding.
2. Daily soaks in briny water.
3. Evening skinny-dipping sessions with your sparring partners.

Well, if you're anything like me, I have not indulged in any of them for the purpose of boxing training. Yes, I have ridden a horse once or twice in my life. I've soaked in briny water if you count trips to the beach. As for the last one, never done it, don't plan on it, don't want to and can't imagine how one would even broach the idea with your sparring partners.

Does that conversation go along these lines?

Good session, your rear hook is a monster today.

Thanks, I was doing everything I could to get inside your jab.

Hey, you know I just thought of something. You know what would really improve our boxing?

What's that?

Me, you, nude in the pool.

Just remembered I've got a thing to be at. Bye.

I bring up the above bizarre training tactics because they are, in fact, actual methods used by three boxing legends. Gentleman Jim Corbett felt that his daily horseback rides toned his organs for the rigors of the ring. Jack Dempsey thought that rubbing brine into his skin would toughen it. Oscar De La Hoya feels that daily skinny-dipping sessions strengthen the bond between himself and his partners. Actually, you could fill a chapter with De La Hoya's unusual approaches, which include non-ejaculatory sex and nude trainer massages with vinegar and select spices. Again, there is no argument concerning the ring prowess of these champions, but I ask you, do you feel the need to saddle up, slap some salty brine on your face or hit the pool with you and your partners all a-danglin'?

I wager most of us will opt for the more mainstream approach to boxing training — the roadwork, the floor work, the bag work, skipping rope, you know, the whole Rocky bit and leave the esoteric stuff out of the

> ... if the predecessor's method is based on a faulty premise, **then** emulating the faulty premise is wheel spinning.

picture. We, the 21st century athletes, can stick with the tried and true. But what if some of the approaches that we think of as tried and true are not necessarily true? What if some of what we take for granted as musts for training are no less quirky and unrelated to boxing as going for a pony ride or going commando in the hot tub with your buds?

The aforementioned champions were/are not insane for their methods, they were/are simply doing what was/is thought correct by at least some of the boxing community at the time. Physical training like all aspects of human behavior is subject to a tradition bias. This tradition bias has us follow in the successful footsteps of those who preceded us, and that is often the wise course of action. Emulating those who have done what you wish to do is a pretty good map of how to get things done. With that in mind, the tradition bias is somewhat double-edged. Meaning, if the predecessor's method is/was sound, emulating it is a good idea. But the tradition bias can also be negative if the predecessor's method is based on a faulty premise, then emulating the faulty premise is wheel spinning.

This book will help you look at the Attribute Demands List required for boxing and allow you to examine every training tool you currently use for improving your boxing and determine whether or not it is the **most effective, efficient** use of your journey to 10,000 hours.

Anyone out there think they can take on a champ in any division today by horseback riding? Probably not. How about nude rub-downs? What percentage of nudity in any form do you think plays in con-structing a champion? I'd wager the percentage hovers around zero. Now, let's take our smug "we know a little more than these guys" attitude to a few other boxing training methods.

Tradition vs. innovation 2

Boxers are known for doing lots and lots of sit-ups to build a strong abdominal girdle for absorbing punishment. Is this the most efficient, effective way to accom-plish this task?

Boxing is practically the only sport (outside of double Dutch competition) that makes skipping rope a main-stay of "building wind." Is this an effective, efficient tool?

Boxers utilize a variety of bags (heavy, speed, double-end, uppercut) to build punching facility. Is bag work an efficient, effective use of time?

Progress in exercise physiology has led the current state of the science to the conclusion that sit-ups (and crunches for that matter) are a remarkably inefficient way to build a strong, resilient core. There are faster, better ways to accomplish this task — we'll get to those later.

Skipping rope is often used to "build wind," i.e. endurance. The rope can be used for this goal, but it can take you only so far. Again, there are faster and more effective methods to accomplish this goal. We must be honest with ourselves. If we choose a less effective, less efficient method over a superior method (which are usually harder by dint of being more intense) we are either succumbing to the tradition bias or shirking the harder work. Some rope work is fine. Skipping rope should be relegated to adding the occasional spice to a "wind building" routine to keep some bounce in the legs.

Work the heavy bag to build power and endurance? Absolutely! Fantastic tool. Work the double-end bag to build reflexes and eye-hand coordination in a manner specific to boxing? Amen! Speed bag work to build endurance in the shoulders and good punching technique? Um, nope. The heavy bag and good focus pad work will build the endurance in the shoulders far more effectively and efficiently than a speed bag session. As for punching form, speed bag technique in no way, shape or form reflects how punches are actually thrown in the ring. Sorry, folks. As fun as speed bags are, they may be the on the list with nude dips with the friends.

This book will help you look at the Attribute Demands List required for boxing and allow you to examine every training tool you currently use for improving your boxing and determine whether or not it is the most effective, efficient use of your journey to 10,000 hours.

There is nothing wrong including an activity or training tool simply for the sake of tradition as long as you are honest with yourself that you are taking time away from a high-yield tool and spinning your wheels in low to zero yield activities to appease some psychological need. I want to help you out of the tradition bias trap where necessary and make sure your precious time is well used and not simply an odd attachment to tradition such as soaking in brine.

Ain't no party like an old school party

I know there are some who have an inordinate fondness for tradition. And to preserve tradition, I have included plenty of old school methods, particularly those that stand the test of utility. Occasionally a side bar will highlight an old school method and are meant to be informative and place some of the ideas into a historical context. Focusing on the sidebars at the expense of the material in the main portions, in my opinion, is not the wisest course of action, but if you like old school, you'll have plenty to work with.

For those disappointed by the absence of specific speed bag material and wish to pursue it further, might I suggest *The Speed Bag Bible* by Alan Kahn, an excellent compendium of material for those who wish to master this device. Again, if you decide to pursue this, keep it in perspective. Think of it as a cool skill to show off akin to juggling, but don't fool yourself thinking that it is an effective use of your boxing training time.

Big and strong or just strong

Don't worry, folks, we're almost to the fun physical stuff. But before we get there, a little yammering about lifting weights. There is a school of thought in boxing that either A) You do not lift weights because they will make you bulky and slow or B) If you do lift weights, lift only light ones for high reps.

The bulky and slow myth first. Everyone remember how slow Evander Holyfield was in his prime because of all his weightlifting? Or outside of boxing, anyone find Olympic class sprinters who lift weights to be slow pokes? Yeah, me neither. Sports science shows us again and again that weight training (the right kind, that is) fosters both strength and speed. That combination sounds like a mighty good thing for boxers, doesn't it?

How about lifting light to moderate weights for high reps? The reasoning behind this is to gain some strength and to prevent gaining size. The general idea is sound on the surface because greater muscle mass can cause an undesired climb in weight class.

Boxing, wrestling, MMA and all other combat sports are weight class dependent. The thinking is the lightest weight class you can make without sacrificing speed and strength is a good idea, hence the light weight/ high reps prescription. But as it turns out, this is not necessarily a good idea after all.

Lifting light weights (no matter the repetition numbers) does not contribute to an appreciable gain in strength. There is an increase in muscular endurance, but this can be accomplished more readily by increasing the weight (this builds strength as well as endurance), shooting for moderate repetitions (the weight increase will not permit high reps) and cycling or circuiting the lifting work so that the lifting wavers between metabolic (endurance/stamina building) and anabolic (muscle building) states.

Circuiting between the two states provides an optimum mixture of efficiency and efficacy. In fact, we cut time by building both stamina and strength simultaneously, while at the same time staving off the upward tick in weight gain. As a matter of fact, upping the weight load and lowering the repetitions while circuiting should provide a weight cutting effect. This sort of approach is ideal for the boxer (and all combat athletes for that matter) and allows the athlete to build maximum optimal fitness in minimum time in his GPP work and devote larger portions of time to the 10,000-hour SPP work.

If the athlete's goal is to go up in weight class, then he can simply add more weight in any given weighted circuit, lower the reps by 1/3 and allow a teensy bit more

> Boxing and all combat sports have the goals of getting **stronger, faster and better** at the heart of their mission statement. Looking great at the beach is low on the list ...

rest time between circuited exercises. We can, of course, tweak bodyweight both upward and downward via diet, a topic we may address in another guide.

OK, assuming we all agree that lifting weights is good for boxing, a brief bit on how to lift.

Counterfeit muscle

Think you'll find preacher bench curls in here? Lat pulldowns? Chest today, quads tomorrow schedules? Nope, absolutely not. Isolation exercises and the "train per body part" method has been so thoroughly debunked in so many sources that I will spend no time on it here. Suffice to say that most any exercise that is used in bodybuilding or that aims to build an aesthetic effect as opposed to a functional athletic expression (form over function) should be avoided and labeled time wasters.

Boxers are performance-based athletes and many possess physiques pleasing to the eye, but these are side effects, not the sought for end result. Boxing and all combat sports have the goals of getting stronger, faster and better at the heart of their mission statement.

So in a nutshell, lift heavy, lift fast and always opt for combination exercises.

Looking great at the beach is low on the list (although, looking great at the beach seems to come with the functional athletic training territory). The old school boxers and wrestlers had a term for those who chose training for show over performance — counterfeit muscle.

You don't want counterfeit muscle, you want legitimate, functional muscle, and there are only three ways to build it.

1. Lift heavy.
2. Focus on combination exercises while always avoiding isolation exercises.
3. Lift explosively.

We discussed lifting heavy in the previous section. Combination exercises means the more of your body that is called upon to lift, the better the exercise (also known as total body lifting). An example of a total body lift is a thruster, a front squat followed by an overhead press. Rather than segmenting/isolating the front squats on one day and the overhead press on another, the combination of the two creates a synergistic effect where the total value of the combined exercise is greater than if the exercises had been executed separately.

As important as lifting heavy and exercise choice (combination lifts) are, you will rapidly and significantly improve your GPP/SPP progress by increasing the rate of lift. When and wherever possible, lift explosively. Lifting slowly trains your muscles to respond slowly whereas lifting explosively trains you to be fast and strong. Think of it this way, would you work the heavy bag in slow motion to build punching power? Of course not, you've got to bring the same intensity to lifting that you do to your SPP work.

So in a nutshell, lift heavy, lift fast and always opt for combination exercises.

Got the groundwork principles down? Of course you do.

Let's go the gym.

Champion's tale #1

Headstands

Kostya Tszyu employed more than a few unusual methods to earn his titles. He would stand on his head in the middle of the ring for approximately three minutes to simply breathe and focus. He would follow this with tumbling around the ring for about 25 revolutions.

Training menus

We separate the workouts into two sections — GPP and SPP. An optimum mix would have you select one choice from the GPP menu, which you perform first, and then one selection from the SPP menu, which is to be worked immediately following the GPP selection. I advise you to never stack GPP choices. That is, don't do one GPP workout followed immediately by a second GPP workout. If you've worked the GPP at optimum intensity, you won't feel like two in a row anyway. But you can stack SPP menu options. SPP menu items are suggested bare minimums that encourage us to always seek marginal improvement each training session. Always feel free to do more SPP work, but never leave gas in the tank for two consecutive GPP sessions.

Exception to the above rule:
If you are prepping for a fight, you may run two GPP sessions in a single day if you adopt a split schedule. That is one GPP session in the morning and a second GPP in the afternoon followed by your SPP option(s).

Regarding the Boxing SPP selections, if there is any question regarding specific technique, please refer to our companion book in this series, *Boxing Mastery*. Ideally, the manual in your hands and *Boxing Mastery* are meant to be used side by side.

GPP vocabularies

Before we construct specific boxing workouts, let's make sure we're all on the same page with the strict exercise forms we'll be using to build our marginal revolution. I urge you to follow the exact guidelines offered for each exercise, even the ones you think you've got a handle on because some old favorites have been tweaked to give you more bang for the buck. We'll separate these exercises according to category and then reconstitute them in the training menus section.

1. Floorwork

Floorwork is boxing parlance for calisthenics or body weight exercises. We'll further subdivide floorwork into pushing, pulling, legs, core (abs/stomach) and medicine ball exercises.

1.1 Pushing floorwork

Hand release push-ups

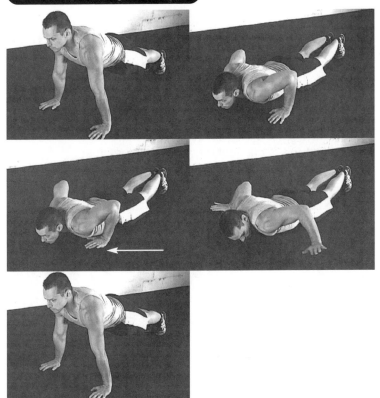

● Everyone knows how to do a push-up, but we introduce the hand release, which makes all push-ups a bit harder.

● At the bottom of each push-up, briefly rest your chest on the floor and lift both hands from the ground.

● This pause lasts no more than a fraction of a second, but it removes muscle elasticity for bounce and forces you to work harder, therefore, get stronger.

● You will use hand release on all push-up varieties when your hands and/or feet are not elevated.

Stacked feet push-ups

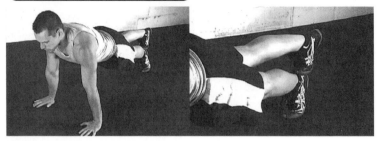

● Place the toe of one foot on the heel of the other.

Wide grip push-ups

● Place your hands two shoulder-widths apart.

Roman push-ups

● Place your hands as wide as you can manage with the fingertips pointing away from your flanks.

Diamond push-ups

● Place your hands beneath your chest with index fingers and thumbs touching.
● No hand release here because your chest should rest on your hands.

Staggered hands push-ups

● Placing your hands in unequal positions adds some unusual stress.

Side-to-side push-ups

● Descend toward your right hand. Hand release and back up.
● Repeat on the left side.

Spiderman push-ups

● At the bottom of the first rep, bring your right knee to your right elbow — no hand release on this one — back up.
● Repeat on the opposite side.

Dive bombers

● Place your feet two shoulder-widths apart.
● Arch your hips to the sky.
● Sweep your chest down and between your arms until your hips brush the floor — no hand release.
● Reverse the motion.

T push-ups

● Perform a push-up.
● As you come up shift all your weight to one hand and turn your body to reach for the sky with the other.
● Repeat on the other side.

Push-up & row

● Perform push-up on dumbbell handles.
● At the top of each push-up, alternate rowing the dumbbells to your chest.
● So it's push-up — row right, push-up — row left.
● That's one rep.

Clapping push-ups

● Be sure to add hand release to make it really fun.

Plate crossover push-ups

● Place your right hand on a weight plate, your left is on the floor.
● Hit a push-up (no hand release) and at the top, hop your body to the other side.
● Left hand will now be on the plate and the right on the floor.
● Repeat.
● That's one rep.

Boardinghouse reach

● Hit the top of a push-up.
● As quickly as possible slap the ground 18 inches in front of you with your right, then return your hand to support position.
● Repeat with the left.
● Optimally you will slap right and left as rapidly as possible.
● If you're sucking wind after 10 reps, you're doing it right.

ISO pause push-ups

● Descend to two inches above the floor and hold for five seconds.
● Rise to the half way mark and hold for five seconds.
● That's one rep.

Decline push-ups

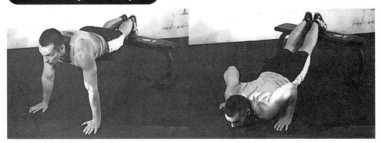

● Place your feet on an elevated surface.
● The higher the surface the greater the difficulty.

Single-leg decline push-ups

● One leg is posted on the elevated surface.
● The other is held aloft.

P push-ups

● Both feet are elevated and the hands are placed on parallel supports that allow you to descend lower than usual.

Jumping push-ups

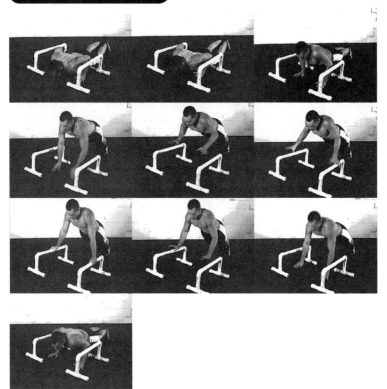

● Perform a hand release push-up between the supports.
● Then burst to land in a push-up on top of them.
● Fall back to the bottom position.

One arm push-ups

● That's right, Rocky style, but use hand release.

Bar dips

● Grip the bars and descend until your elbows exceed 90 degrees of bend.

Weighted bar dips

● Add a weight belt to make it more fun.

Ring dips

● Descend until your armpits touch
the tops of the rings.

Half cross / ring dip combo

● At the top of each ring dip…
● Keep your arms straight and slowly extend your arms away from your body.
● Bring them back in. Now hit your dip.

Handstand push-ups

● Kick against a wall (or walk your feet up).
● Descend until your forehead touches the floor.

Handstand kongs

● Hit your handstand.
● Shift your weight to your right and then touch your chest with your left hand.
● Repeat on the other side. ● That's one rep.

Handstand walk-ups

● Place two weight plates on the floor.
● Hit your handstand between them.
● Walk your right hand to one plate, then your left to the other. ● That's one rep.

Champion's tale #2

Bag bar

Ricky "The Hitman" Hatton used a grueling circuit dubbed Bag Bar. A bar approximately waist high was placed near the heavy bag station. He would jump back and forth over the bar for one minute, then bang the bag for one minute, then return to the bar for the third minute of the round.

1.2 Pulling floorwork

Inverted row

● Keeping your body straight, pull until your chest touches the bar.

Inverted row underhand grip

● The same as the preceding but with an under-hand grip.

Inverted row feet elevated

● You know what to do.

Inverted row underhand grip / feet elevated

● Ditto.

Inverted rows side to side

● Pull toward one hand and then the other.
● That's one rep.

Inverted row single arm punch

● Burst from the bottom and punch the right arm to the sky.
● Descend and repeat with the left.

Inverted row rings

● The same exercises performed with rings take away some stability and add to the difficulty.

Pull-ups

● Hit a full dead hang with zero flex in shoulder or elbows.
● Pull until the chin is above the bar.
● You will use the full dead hang protocol on all pull-up/chin-up varieties.

Pull-ups wide grip

● Take a grip two shoulder-widths apart on the bar.

Chin-ups

● Use an underhand grip on the bar.

Chin-ups close grip

● Take an underhand grip approximately eight inches apart.

Baseball pull-ups

● Place one hand in an overgrip and the other in an undergrip.
● When pulling, do not allow the body to twist.
● Perform prescribed repetitions, then switch grips and repeat.

Pull rights / lefts

● Pull up taking your chin to your right hand and then the left hand for the next repetition.

Towel pull-ups

- This one is excellent for the grip.
- Throw a towel over the bar and hit your reps.

Ring pull-ups

- Useful for the lack of stability.

Clapping hands pull-ups

● This one is excellent for explosive power.
● Burst to the top of the bar...
● Hit a quick release and clap your hands.
● Re-grasp and descend.

Weighted pull-ups

● Strap on a weight vest and go.

Weighted chin-ups

● Ditto

1.3 Legs floorwork

You'll find more legwork in Chapter 2, Plyometrics work.

Zombie squats

● Put your arms in front of you.
● Keep flat-footed and drop until your butt is eight inches off the floor.

Prisoner squats

● Place your hands behind your head with elbows pulled back.
● Descend to eight inches.

Prisoner jump squats

● At the top of each squat jump 8-12 inches.

Steering wheel squats

● Hold a weight plate extended in front of your body throughout.

Champion's tale #3

Dancing balls

Kostya Tszyu used a tennis ball suspended from an elastic cord attached to a headband. He would punch at the dangling tennis ball seeking to keep it dancing away from him in a steady rhythm.

Burpees

● Drop to a squat ...
● Place both hands on the floor and shoot your legs back into push-up position.
● Drop and hit one hand release push-up.
● Return to the squat.
● Jump 8-12 inches, clapping your hands overhead.

Single-leg burpee

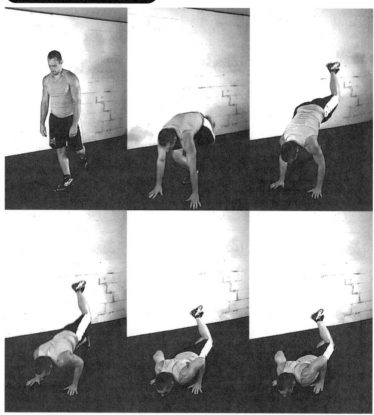

● The same as before, but hit all reps using only the right leg and then repeat with the left leg.

Pistols, aka single-leg squats

● Hold one leg in front of you.
● Stay flat-footed and descend until your butt is eight inches off the floor.
● Once the right leg reps are completed, work the left.

1.4 Core floorwork / Roman chair exercises

You will notice no crunches or sit-ups. Why? Exercise science demonstrates that they are highly inefficient for building abdominal/core strength. You'll find the following substitutions grueling enough.

Reverse hip raise

● Rest your abs on the support.
● Raise your hips/legs as one unit until parallel with the floor.

Bent knee reverse hip raise

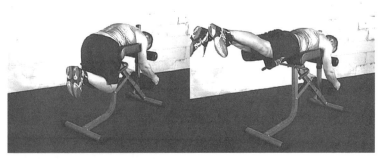

● Prepare as you did in the preceding, but the legs begin in a 90 degree bend and then extended to parallel.

Back extension

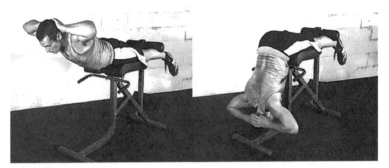

● Place your pelvis on the support and bend your body 90 degrees.
● Return to parallel.

1.5 True floorwork

A good target for each version of the plank is a strict two-minute hold.

Plank

● Keeping your body straight, balance on your toes and both elbows for the prescribed time.

Plank single leg

● Hold one leg aloft throughout.

Plank single arm extended

● Keeping your body straight, balance on your toes and elbows for the prescribed time.

Plank single arm & leg

● Lift and extend opposite limbs. For example, lift right arm and left leg.

Side plank

● Rest on one elbow as you support along your body's flank.

Single-leg side plank (top leg lifted)

● The photo is worth more than my words.

Single-leg side plank (bottom leg tucked)

● Ditto.

Mountain climbers

● Support your weight on your hands and quickly jump the right knee to the right elbow …
● Repeat on the other side.
● That's one.

Grasshoppers

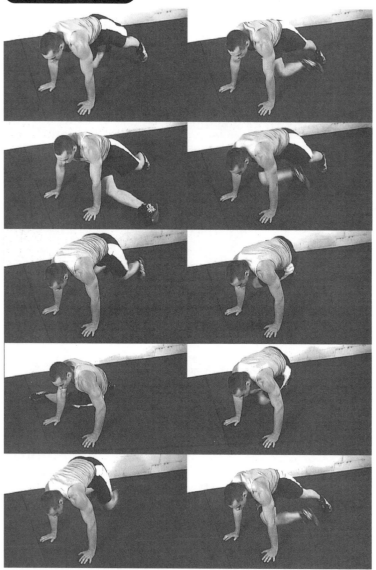

● Essentially an opposite limb mountain climber.
● Right knee to left elbow and vice versa.

Barbell rollout

- Get on your knees and grip a loaded barbell.
- Roll the barbell away from you until just at the point of collapse.
- Use your core to roll the barbell back.

Bicycles

● Lie on the floor with your hands behind your head.
● Crunch upper back off the floor and bring your right elbow to your left knee.
● Repeat on the other side for one rep.

Hanging leg raise (toes to bar)

● Hang from the bar and bring your toes up to touch the bar.

Knees to elbows

● Bet you know what to do.

Hanging hurdle

● Place a 24-inch barrier perpendicular before you.
● Hang from the bar keeping your legs straight. Touch down first to the right of the hurdle and then to the left for one rep.

Sledgehammer

Sledge work (wielding a sledgehammer) and/or chopping wood are old school boxing staples to build some serious core snap into punches. We offer the following varieties. You can actually chop wood or use a sledge on an old tire or sandbag. I suggest using a sledge with at least a 16-pound head.

Sledgehammer variations

From both knees.   From one knee.

1.6 Medicine ball floorwork

The medicine ball is an old school tool that still has a good deal of utility behind it.

Medicine ball push-ups two on one

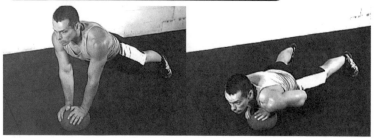

● Two hands on the ball.

Medicine ball push-ups one on one

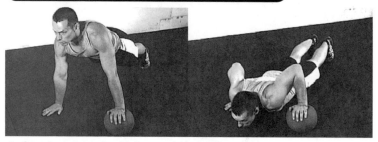

● One hand on the ball, one hand off.

Medicine ball mountain climbers two on one

● Bet you know what to do.

Medicine ball grasshoppers two on one

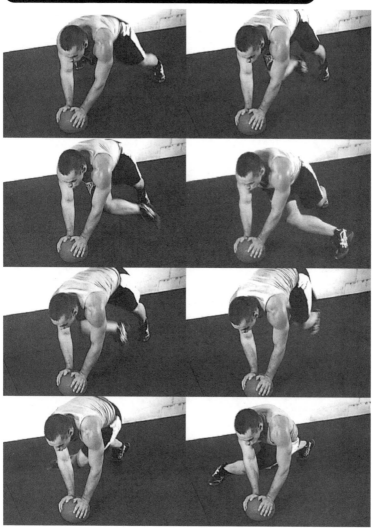

● Ditto.

V-ups

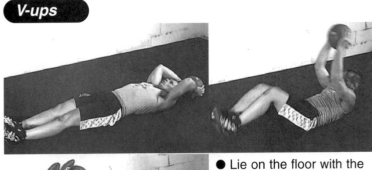

● Lie on the floor with the ball extended above your head.
● Snap your legs and upper body from the mat as if you were going to slam the ball into your toes.

Push pass

● Use a two-hand push to toss the ball to your partner.

Side throw

● Use a scooping motion to toss the ball.
● Match reps on the opposite side.

Granny toss

● Underhand for distance.

Backward toss

● Underhand throw the ball overhead for distance.

Pullover pass

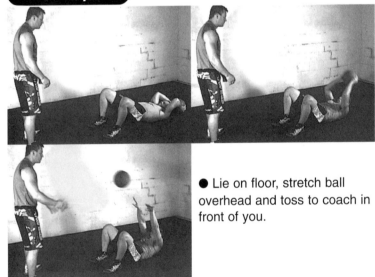

● Lie on floor, stretch ball overhead and toss to coach in front of you.

Gut check and push pass

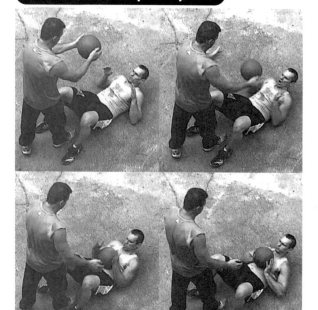

● Your partner drops the ball on your tightened abs.

● You absorb the impact with a forceful exhalation of breath and push pass it back.

Ball slams

● Using a slam ball (an indestructible, nonbouncing medicine ball), extend the ball overhead and then slam it into the ground with great power.

Ball relay and body sprint
● You can use any of the preceding tosses for distance with a slam ball and then sprint to the ball and repeat.

2. Plyometrics work

While not strictly floorwork or weight work, the following exercises will build explosiveness in the lower body more quickly and effectively than skipping rope. A 24-inch plyo box and a 24-inch hurdle or two can add a great deal of explosiveness to your punching base. Think of these two pieces of gear as the lower body equivalent of the medicine ball.

Barrier hops

● Use a 24-inch hurdle to jump from side to side.

Hurdle jumps

● Jump forward over the hurdle.

Standing broad jump

● Always go for maximum distance.

Box jumps

● Jump to the top of a 24-inch box.
● Always land with feet toward the center of the box and come to a full stand before stepping down.

Lateral box jumps

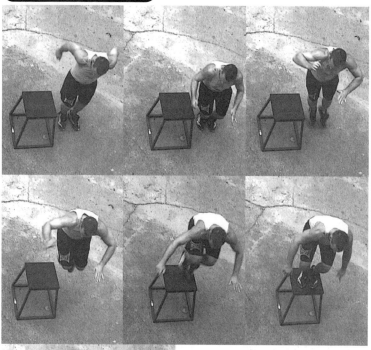

● Standing sideways to the box, hit your box jumps.

Depth jumps

● Jump from the box landing in a deep squat. Then jump a second time as high as you can into the air.

Champion's tale #4

Killer sit-ups

Nigel "The Dark Destroyer" Benn utilized stand-up/sit-ups in his routine. First he'd sit on the floor and have his coach anchor his feet. When he hit the peak of the sit-up, he'd continue to a standing position.

Box burpees

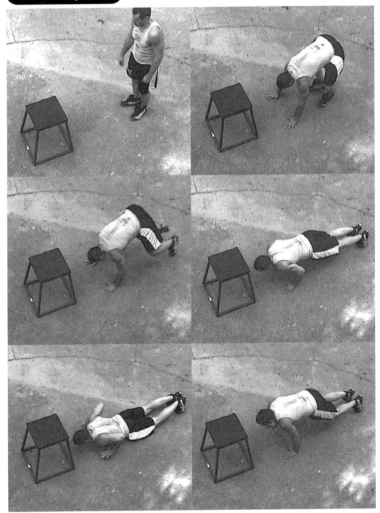

● Stand in front of the box.
● Perform a burpee complete with hand release push-up. At the jump portion, jump onto the box.

Over box jumps

● Jump over the plyo box.

3. Weight work

Yes, we've already included some weight gear in the floorwork section but, here, we get into the weight work being the focus of the work as opposed to serving as an assist to the floorwork. To get the most out of weight work for boxing (or any combat sport for that matter), we should abide by the following guidelines.

1. Train unsupported. This means, whenever and wherever possible, stay away from machines. Machines, by definition, are there to make work easier for human beings. Machines support the body, machines keep the weights in strict paths of movement, machines supply stability in most ranges of motion. In other words, machines remove vital aspects that make the human body stronger faster. For those who doubt this pronouncement, find your max weight on a leg press machine, then see how you do with an actual back squat. Or test your Universal machine bench press against a free weight bench press. Machines are ego-stroking conveniences. Leave them behind and let real work do the stroking for you.

... machines remove vital aspects that make the human body stronger faster.

2. Train with free weights whenever and wherever possible. If possible choose Olympic weights and Olympic bars over standard free weights. Free weights challenge the body by recruiting secondary and tertiary muscle groups to stabilize the primary groups. Oh, and one more time, no machines.

Even though you use free weights with a Smith machine, it's still a machine. Beyond a power rack and a bench for the occasional bench press, all you need are your O-Bar and your plates.

> Lifting for combat sports should be reflective of how these sports are played.

3. Be a weight thrower not a weight lifter. Lifting for combat sports should be reflective of how these sports are played. Punches are thrown with explosive bad intentions, not slow-motion versions of Arnie biceps curl pumps. By emphasizing explosiveness over slow lifting, we also build a staggering amount of metabolic conditioning. Anyone who thinks weight training can't be a cardiovascular endurance builder simply has never lifted correctly.

4. Don't be a bodybuilder. Don't train for aesthetics, train for performance. Always choose function over form. In other words, no biceps curls when there is a clean and jerk to be done. The boxer has no need to train isolated body parts. The boxer needs the body to work as a whole, so emphasize compound lifts that call on as many body parts as possible. For example, the back squat is a fantastic strength builder, but the front squat might be more ideal as it loads the shoulders, the back, the core, as well as the legs (the extra effort is why front squat totals are lower than back squat totals—it's harder work).

Also, don't fall into the bodybuilder trap of "Chest today/Legs tomorrow." You are not a bodybuilder, you are an athlete aiming to be the best boxer you can be who has no need for isolation exercises or body-part circuits. To put it another way, as a boxer, if you punch today in training does not mean you can't punch tomorrow. Of course you can. Throw this outmoded thinking away.

5. Go single limb occasionally. Remember what we said about not using machines? Well, an Olympic bar is not a machine, but it is a tool, and tools serve the same purpose as machines — to make work a little easier. Try this experiment to prove it to yourself. Find a weight that you can bench press comfortably for five reps. For arguments sake, let's say its 225 pounds. Theoretically, you've benched 112.5 pounds in each hand. Do you think you can grab two 110-pound dumbbells and knock out five reps just as easily? I'm sure you know the answer.

> Dumbbells add instability (that's good) and reveal weaknesses across symmetry (also good).

Bars are tools. We need them, but it is wise to occasionally perform the standard lifts with dumbbells. Dumbbells add instability (that's good) and reveal weaknesses across symmetry (also good). Dumbbell lifting, whether single or double, can correct these weaknesses and build a stronger, better fighter.

6. Body weight is a mighty fine goal. Boxing (and all combat sports for that matter) is a weight class dependent sport. Ideally, the competitive fighter will come in at the top end of the lowest weight class he can manage while preserving as much strength and mass as he can. A fighter who walks around comfortably as a middleweight might want to cut to welter so he can be stronger in that class as opposed to facing natural light-heavies who cut to his own walk-around middleweight.

With an eye on preserving as many physical attributes as we can without increasing our natural weight so much that weight cutting becomes a bigger chore than it already is, the combat athlete might want to use his own body weight as the primary weight goal. That is, rather than strive for ever higher poundages on bench presses or back squats, we might be better served to preserve reasonable weight class if we target loads that approximate our body weight as the upper end more often than not. Of course, the occasional push above is perfectly acceptable and useful, but we must not lose sight of the fact that we are preparing for boxing not Olympic weight lifting or power lifting competitions.

You're job is to attack these weights with the same intensity that you would an opponent.

7. Push! You are a fighter. You have already chosen a vocation/avocation that is tougher than most things the majority will ever do or even attempt. Bring this same toughness to your weight training. Do not read the sets and reps within the GPP menus as a license to do a few reps, then walk around, hit the water fountain, waste time.

You're a fighter. You're job is to attack these weights with the same intensity that you would an opponent. If you finish any GPP workout and are not gasping for breath at the end, you A) Went too light and need to up the weight on the next session or B) Went too slow. Doesn't matter which one, A or B, they both add up to spinning your wheels. You're in the gym to train, not pose. If you're not there to push yourself, you might need to reevaluate what it is you want to do. Maybe boxing ain't for you.

Assuming it is, let's have a look at the weight exercises. BTW, this is not meant to be an encyclopedia on every weight exercise there is. This is a rundown of compound lifts that are of utmost value to the boxer.

3.1 Bar work

Bench press

● I think we all know how to do this one.

Close grip bench press

● Bring your grip hands to approximately eight inches apart.

Reverse grip bench press

● Take an undergrip on the bar.

Bent row

● Pull the bar from the floor until it touches your diaphragm.

Press

● With no assist from the legs, press the bar overhead.

Champion's tale #5

Lung bursters

Ken "The Tartan Legend" Buchanan's favorite exercise was swimming. He felt that swimming underwater while holding his breath until he thought his lungs would burst was beneficial to his middleweight success.

Push press

● Here you can use the leg assist of a half squat to pop higher weight overhead.

Clean

● Take an overgrip on the bar and burst it from the ground to just below your chin.

Clean & jerk

● Clean the bar and then use a leg assisted jump to press the weight overhead.

Hang clean

● Holding the weight at hang position (arms extended, weight resting on thighs) …
● Aggressively pop the hips and clean the bar.

Squat clean

● This time when you clean the bar, jump under it landing in a squat position.

● Then perform a front squat to come to a standing clean.

Power curl

● Essentially an under-hand clean.

Snatch

- Take grip two shoulder-widths apart.
- Leaving the arms straight, perform an aggressive jump shrugging the bar along with you.
- At the apex of the shrug, transition the weight to overhead.

Back squat

● Rack the bar on your back.
● Squat to eight inches.

Front squat

● Rack the bar in clean position and hit the eight-inch target.

Zercher squats

● Rack the bar in the crooks of your arms this time.

Overhead squats

● This one is tough, tough, tough so start with low weight.
● Hold the bar overhead, arms straight.
● Hit your eight-inch target.
● Have fun!

Barbell jump squats

● Rack the bar on your back.
● At the top of each squat, execute a jump of 6-8 inches.

Dead lift

● You get to load the bar heavy here.
● Take an overgrip on the bar.
● Start with the bar close to your shins and think sit-back as you extend your legs and back.

Thrusters

● Simply a front squat combined with a push press, but this one demands some serious lung power.

3.2 Dumbbell work

Many of these are simply correlates of barbell work. We describe only the single exercise that is unique.

Dumbbell bench press

Single-arm bench press

Single-arm row

Dumbbell press

Single-arm press

Goblet squat

● Grip the underside of the top bell of a vertically held dumbbell and hit your squats.

Dumbbell thrusters

3.3 Kettlebell work

This old school piece of gear has returned to the fore-
front of conditioning methods and for good reason. It's
a versatile tool because it demands total body effort.
Beyond the following described exercises, you can perform all single-hand exercises described in the
Dumbbell Work section with a single kettlebell.

Two-hand swing

● Grip the handle of the kettlebell with both hands.
● Use an aggressive forward pop of the hips and fire the kettlebell to approximately eye level.

One-hand swing

Turkish get-up

● Lie on the floor and grip the kettlebell in one hand.
● Hold it aloft as if you've performed a single-arm bench press from the floor.
● Keeping the kettlebell overhead throughout, rise onto your free hand and hip.
● Bring yourself to standing.
● That's a single rep.

Snatch

● Use a big jump burst to bring the kettlebell from the floor to overhead with no pauses in the transition.

4. GPP menus

We provide 31 separate GPP workouts. They are meant to be attacked in a random manner, meaning that you can follow them in an A-Z order and then start over again, or mix and match as you see fit. Once the form is understood, you can use the exercise vocabulary section to create your own, or you can visit our Web site for new GPP menus posted weekly: www.extremeselfprotection.com

GPP Legend

Levels
The menus are adjusted for three levels of conditioning:
1. Advanced/professional
2. Intermediate (You've got at least six months of hard conditioning under your belt.)
3. Rookies

Poundage
With that in mind, suggested poundage is offered for the three levels (in parentheses). Occasionally there are suggested rounds for the levels. Feel free to scale upward or downward as need be for your specific needs.

Countdown
Each round you perform one less rep of the given exercise. For example, 10 reps in round 1, then nine reps, all the way down to one rep.

10/40s

Set a 50-yard course with a marker at the first 10 yards. You will perform whatever task is set for the first 10 yards and then burst immediately into a 40-yard sprint. Jog back and repeat the given task.

Shuttle

Shuttle means to sprint the distance both ways. That is, to shuttle 40 yards is to sprint 40 yards, touch the line and immediately sprint back 40 yards.

Onto the menus ...

GPP 1

50 yard sprints X 10
- 30 seconds of rest between.
- Score completed sprints in 10 minutes.

GPP 2

Two miles. Run your fastest two miler.

GPP 3

a. Bench press (225/200/body weight) 3
b. Slam ball toss relay (40/30/20) 40 yards. Throw the ball as far as you can, sprint to it and repeat for the remaining distance.
c. Slam ball 40 yards. Pick up the ball and sprint back.
X 10

GPP 4

a. Travelling prisoner jump squats 20 yards
b. Bear crawl 20 yards
c. Clean (135/125/105) 10
X 5

GPP 5
a. Bench press (body weight) 15
b. Goblet squat (50/45/40) 30
X 5

GPP 6
Barbell thrusters (135/125/105) 50
● Sprint 50 yards each time you set the bar down.

GPP 7
a. Bent rows (body weight) 10
b. Mountain climbers 10
c. Handstand step-ups 10
X 10

GPP 8
a. Single-leg burpees 10 (alternate legs each round)
b. Handstand push-ups 5
X 10

GPP 9
a. Bicycle V-ups 10
b. Ring dips
X 10

GPP 10
a. Single-arm dumbbell bench press (60/50/40) 5 per arm
b. Barbell rollouts 8
c. Broad jump 10/40
X 10

GPP 11
a. Boardinghouse reach 10
b. Push press (135/125/115) 5
c. Bear crawl start 10/40
● Bear crawl on all fours for the first 10 yards then sprint the remaining 40 yards.
X10

GPP 12
a. Prisoner squats 20
b. Handstand push-ups 10
Complete rounds in 25 minutes.

GPP 13
a. Clapping pull-ups 5
b. Bar dips 10
c. Box jump 10
d. Clapping push-ups 10
X 10

GPP 14
a. Pull-ups 40
b. 40-yard sprint
c. Prisoner squats 40
d. 40-yard sprint
e. Push-ups 40
f. 40-yard sprint
X 2

GPP 15
a. Dumbbell thrusters (50/45/40) 10
b. 200 yards
Advanced: 8 rounds / Intermediate: 6 rounds / Rookies: 4 rounds

GPP 16
a. P push-ups 10
b. Pull-ups 10
c. 40-yard shuttle
X 10

GPP 17
a. Dead lift (body weight) Your body weight in reps
b. 50-yard shuttle per drop

GPP 18
a. Pull-ups 10
b. Push-ups 10
c. Skip rope one minute (doubles)
X 10

GPP 19
a. Dead lift (225/200/185)
b. Bear start 10/40s
c. Countdown dead lift from 10

GPP 20
a. Prisoner squats 50
200 yards
b. Prisoner squats 40
200 yards
c. Prisoner squats 30
200 yards
d. Prisoner squats 20
200 yards
e. Prisoner squats 10
200 yards

GPP 21
a. Dumbbell thrusters (50/45/40)
b. Bear crawl 40
c. Reverse bear crawl 40
d. Countdown thrusters

GPP 22
a. Pistols 5 (both legs)
b. Push press (155/135/115) 10
X 5

GPP 23
a. Front squats (135/125/115) 5
b. Push-up dumbbell row (30/25/15) 10
c. Over box jump — sprint 15 yards
X 10

GPP 24
a. Knees to elbows 10
b. Broad jumps (6-foot minimum)
X 10

GPP 25
a. Front squats (body weight)
b. Handstand kongs
Countdown both from 10

GPP 26
a. Kettlebell triplet (70/60/50)
● The triplet is a two-hand swing, followed by a single-arm swing right-handed, and then a single-arm swing left-handed. That's one rep.
b. Iron cross / ring dip combo
Countdown both from 10

GPP 27
a. Hang clean (body weight or best approximation) 3
b. Burpee box jump 10
X 5

GPP 28
a. Kettlebell swings (70/60/50) 10
b. 50-yard shuttle
X 10

GPP 29
a. Hanging hurdle 10
b. Jumping push-ups 10
X 10

GPP 30
a. Barbell jump squats (body weight)
b. 50-yard shuttle
c. Countdown squats

GPP 31
a. Jumping prisoner squats
b. Clapping push-ups
Countdown both from 10

Champion's tale #6

Max ISOs

Ken Buchanan also used barbell pullover isometric holds:

● Lie on the floor and reach your arms above your head.

● Grasp a barbell 6 inches off the floor.

● Hold this position until you have to drop it.

● Rest for 15 seconds and repeat.

5. Boxing SPP choices

The boxing SPP Choices are broken into sections according to which piece of gear or skill of focus is featured. You will find two approaches within each section — the Old School and the New School.

The Old School choices are informed by the Champions' Bell Curve[1], a loose survey of the approximate number of rounds put into said skill/equipment per session by champions of the past and present. The New School choices are based upon the current state of conditioning science and the "Gaming the Gear" protocol. What exactly is Gaming the Gear?

Gaming the Gear

Smart approaches to solo combat training gear involve tweaking a few elements to make sure that our practice is never rote. These approaches push us to build new skills and better conditioning. There are essentially two ways to tweak solo gear training. The first is the more common method of technique honing — using prescripted combinations and skills and then grooving them into your neuromuscular net. The second approach involves Gaming the Gear.

Gaming the Gear is imposing artificial guidelines, time limits and even an arbitrary scoring system onto your training. Gaming the Gear allows you to turn up the competitive heat among training partners even when not sparring and/or allows you to qualitatively and quantitatively chart progress even if you are training solo. We use both approaches in this manual.

1. The germ of the idea for the Champions' Bell Curve came from *Workouts from Boxing's Greatest Champs* by Gary Todd.

A brief word on mechanics

We now move to how to use boxing specific gear and various drills to apply to these tools. This manual operates on the assumption that you already have good technique under your belt to apply to said pieces of gear, and we will spend no time on how to punch, how to move and so on. If you do not already have good technique or suspect that you may have a few areas that need brushing up, I suggest using the companion manual in this series, *Boxing Mastery*. Use it as a side-by-side adjunct to this material.

5.1 Footwork tango

Smart feet, smart fighter. We've heard that bit of
wisdom from boxing trainers for ages. The phrase has
been around for ages because it's true. Top fighters
know footwork is key. But we also know footwork isn't
as fun/dramatic as working punches. Nevertheless, YOU
MUST HAVE GOOD FOOTWORK TO BE A GOOD
BOXER.

To combat the tendency to avoid footwork, we offer
the following drill set. Followed precisely, it comprises
all the major aspects of boxing footwork and can be
worked as one continuously looped footwork drill for
rounds and/or (and I highly advise working it this
second way) taking pieces of the tango and applying
them in both your gear and focused sparring work.

Ideally, you will learn the Footwork Tango piece by
piece, giving yourself three three-minute rounds on
each aspect to hone the skill. Once you have it down
pat, you can run it as a whole or pull it apart and
reassemble pieces for new drill sets.

Slow advance X 3

● Step and drag forward three steps.
● Always move the foot closest to the direction you are moving first. (Here, the lead foot steps forward and the rear drags to follow).

Slow retreat X 3

● Step and drag to the rear three steps.

Quick advance

● One fast step forward.

Quick retreat & pivot inside

● One quick step to the rear.
● While moving back, cover the liver with the lead hand.
● Step the rear foot 45 degrees and to your inside (toward your chest).
● Pivot on your lead foot back to stance.

Slow outside lateral X 3

● Three steps to the outside (toward your back).

Slow inside lateral X 3

● Three steps toward your inside (toward your chest).

Quick outside lateral & pivot outside

● Quick step out-
side followed by a
pivot toward your
back.

Back & in

● Quick bounce out of range and then back in.

In & out

● The reverse of the above.

In & out pivot outside

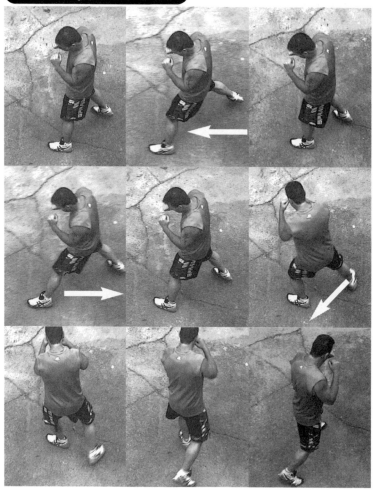

In & out pivot inside

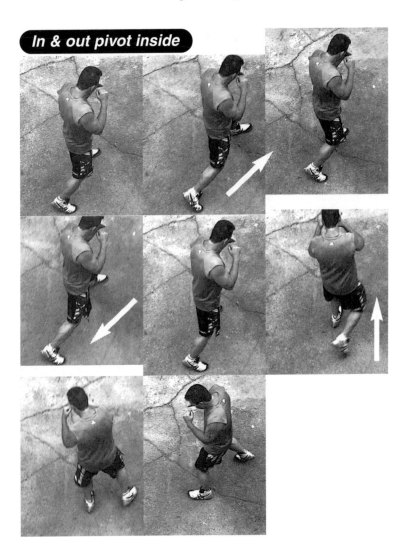

Shift sidestep & pivot

● Drag the lead foot back and then step the rear foot to the inside and pivot back toward the lead foot.

Drop shift X 2

- Hit a half squat on both legs.
- Drag the lead foot back approximately 8-10 inches.
- Step the rear foot to the lead position and stand up.
- Repeat to reverse the stance again.

Rear shift & pivot

- Use this one to clear danger completely.
- Drag the lead foot toward the rear foot.
- Take a big step back with the rear and circle/walk away.

5.2 Combination menu

Use the following combination choices in both gear work and focused sparring work.

TWO-POINT COMBINATIONS

- DOUBLE JAB HEAD
- JAB HEAD / JAB BODY
- JAB BODY / JAB HEAD
- DOUBLE JAB BODY
- JAB HEAD / CROSS HEAD
- JAB HEAD / CROSS BODY
- JAB BODY / CROSS HEAD
- JAB BODY / CROSS BODY
- JAB HEAD / LEAD HOOK HEAD
- JAB BODY / LEAD HOOK HEAD
- JAB BODY / REAR HOOK HEAD
- JAB HEAD / LEFT UPPERCUT
- JAB HEAD / RIGHT UPPERCUT
- LEFT UPPERCUT / JAB HEAD
- CROSS HEAD / LEAD HOOK HEAD
- CROSS BODY / LEAD HOOK HEAD
- CROSS HEAD / LEAD HOOK BODY
- DOUBLE LEAD HOOKS — LOW TO HIGH
  Drop the hand 45 degrees after the low hook to muscle-load the second hook.
- DOUBLE REAR HOOK — LOW TO HIGH
- LEAD HOOK HEAD / LEFT UPPERCUT
- LEAD HOOK HEAD / CROSS BODY
- LEFT UPPERCUT / REAR HOOK HEAD
- LEFT UPPERCUT / RIGHT UPPERCUT

- RIGHT UPPERCUT / LEAD HOOK HEAD
- RIGHT UPPERCUT / CROSS HEAD
- RIGHT UPPERCUT / JAB HEAD
- LEAD HOOK HEAD / REAR HOOK HEAD
- LEAD HOOK HEAD / RIGHT UPPERCUT
- REAR HOOK HEAD / RIGHT UPPERCUT
- RIGHT UPPERCUT / REAR HOOK HEAD

THREE-POINT COMBINATIONS

- TRIPLE JAB
- JAB HEAD / STEP / LEAD HOOK HEAD
- JAB HEAD / LEAD HOOK HEAD / LEFT UPPERCUT
- JAB HEAD / LEFT UPPERCUT / LEAD HOOK HEAD
- JAB HEAD / JAB HEAD / CROSS HEAD
- JAB HEAD / JAB BODY / LEAD HOOK HEAD
- JAB HEAD / CROSS HEAD / LEAD HOOK HEAD
- JAB HEAD / CROSS HEAD / LEFT UPPERCUT
- JAB HEAD / LEAD HOOK HEAD / REAR HOOK HEAD
- CROSS HEAD / LEAD HOOK HEAD/ CROSS HEAD
- LEAD HOOK HEAD / CROSS HEAD / LEAD HOOK HEAD
- LEAD HOOK HEAD / LEFT UPPERCUT / CROSS HEAD
- LEAD HOOK HEAD / LEFT UPPERCUT / REAR HOOK HD.
- LEAD HOOK BODY / LEAD HOOK HEAD / RIGHT UPCUT
- JAB HEAD / CROSS BODY / LEAD HOOK HEAD
- JAB HEAD / CROSS HEAD / JAB HEAD
- JAB HEAD / RIGHT UPPERCUT / HOOK HEAD
- JAB HEAD / LEAD HOOK HEAD / CROSS HEAD
- JAB HEAD / LEAD HOOK HEAD / RIGHT UPPERCUT
- JAB HEAD/ LEAD HOOK BODY / LEAD HOOK HEAD
- JAB HEAD / LEFT UPPERCUT / REAR HOOK HEAD
- LEFT UPPERCUT / REAR HOOK HEAD / LEAD HOOK HD.

FOUR-POINT COMBINATIONS

- JAB HEAD / CROSS HEAD / LEAD HOOK BODY / REAR UPPERCUT

- CROSS HEAD / LEAD HOOK HEAD / CROSS HEAD / LEAD HOOK BODY

- CROSS HEAD / LEAD HOOK HEAD / CROSS BODY / LEAD UPPERCUT

- JAB HEAD / LEAD HOOK HEAD / CROSS HEAD / LEAD HOOK HEAD

- JAB HEAD / LEAD HOOK BODY / LEAD HOOK HEAD / REAR UPPERCUT

- JAB HEAD / CROSS BODY / LEAD HOOK HEAD / REAR HOOK BODY

- JAB HEAD / CROSS HEAD / LEAD SHOVEL HOOK BODY/ REAR SHOVEL HOOK BODY

- LEAD HOOK HEAD / REAR HOOK HEAD / LEFT UPPERCUT / REAR UPPERCUT

- LEFT UPPERCUT / LEAD HOOK HEAD / RIGHT UPPERCUT / REAR HOOK HEAD

- LEAD HOOK HEAD / LEFT UPPERCUT / REAR HOOK HEAD / RIGHT UPPERCUT

- LEAD HOOK HEAD / RIGHT UPPERCUT / LEFT UPPERCUT / REAR HOOK HEAD

FIVE-POINT COMBINATIONS

● JAB HEAD / CROSS HEAD / LEFT UPPERCUT / CROSS HEAD / LEAD HOOK HEAD

● LEAD HOOK / CROSS HEAD / LEFT UPPERCUT / REAR HOOK HEAD / LEAD HOOK BODY

● JAB HEAD / JAB HEAD / CROSS HEAD / LEAD HOOK HEAD / CROSS HEAD

SIX-POINT COMBINATIONS

● JAB HEAD / CROSS HEAD / LEAD HOOK HEAD / CROSS HEAD / LEFT UPPERCUT / RIGHT UPPERCUT

● JAB HEAD / CROSS HEAD / LEFT UPPERCUT / CROSS HEAD / LEAD HOOK HEAD / RIGHT UPPERCUT

Champion's tale #7

Gut busters

Wayne "The Pocket Rocket" McCullough would hold a 20-pound plate behind his head, sit on an exercise ball and perform sit-ups. He felt that the instability provided by the ball built a stronger core.

5.3 Roadwork

To the boxer, running, jogging, sprinting — whatever you call it — whether on an actual road, track or treadmill is called roadwork. Roadwork is a hallmark of boxing training used to condition both the legs and build stamina. We offer two tacks in this section. The Old School way of long, hard miles, and the New School way, which utilizes sprinting intervals to do the same job better in less time (that is, if you trust the science). If you're a traditionalist, plug in the iPOD and hit the road. If you're ready to let science assist your work, plunge into the New School approach. Or mix and match the Old and New to your heart's content. Keep in mind, the less time spent on roadwork the more time you can devote to the 10,000 hours of boxing mark. But please don't use this as an excuse to shirk roadwork or hold back. Old School regimen is between 20-40 miles per week. New School requires 100 percent effort. If you're not pushing hard, you're spinning your wheels and fooling no one but yourself.

Old School roadwork

This is an easy one.

1. Lace up your shoes.
2. Hit the road.
3. Run.
4. Repeat 4-5 days per week.

You're probably wondering just how much to run. Well, in a survey of champions' mileage (both past and current champs) we can see a definite preference for the 3-8 mile range. A loose bell curve distribution puts the mileage as follows:

1-2 miles per day	0%
3-4 miles per day	8%
4-5 miles per day	47%
6-8 miles per day	45%
9-plus miles per day	0%

So, if you wanna do Old School roadwork, ballpark your daily totals in the 4-8 mile range. Oh, and one more thing — the overwhelming majority of these miles are outside, not on tracks or treadmills. Hills are highly encouraged.

New School roadwork

If this is the way you choose to go, simply pick any of the following New School roadwork workouts and plug that into your daily roadwork session. It's best to rotate through these templates and not stand pat on the one or two that you feel good about.

New School —
100% effort

You will also find many of the GPP Exercise Menu workouts feature running. The suggested attack is to alternate between New School roadwork one day and a GPP choice for your conditioning the next day. Of course, if you've got the time for split sessions (morning and evening workouts) feel free to run both in a single day.

New School roadwork gear
● You
● Shoes
● Stopwatch x 2
● Cones
● Measurement Tool — A good way to measure distance if you are not using a clearly demarcated track or field is a measuring wheel such as the kind used by surveyors. You can pick one up at Home Depot or any good supply store.

New School roadwork rules
Just one rule — 100 percent, all-out effort always.

12 New School roadwork (NSR) workouts

NSR 1. Suicide runs
Mark a course as follows: 0 yards (starting line), 10 yards, 20 yards, 30 yards, 40 yards and 50 yards.
● Start an overall timer and sprint to the 10 and touch the line with your right hand, sprint back to zero and touch.
● Repeat the process going to the 20, then the 30, 40 and 50.
● Once you sprint through the line returning from the 50, rest for a strict 60 seconds.
● Repeat this process for a total of three rounds.
● Score your performance with your overall timer (rest times are included in the total), which is left running from the first sprint until the final.
● Chart this time and when this workout pops up again, strive to match or beat your previous time.
● If you come in five seconds slower hit one more round.

NSR 2. 10/50s
● Run a series of 10 50-yard dashes with a strict 30 seconds of rest between efforts.
● Score your overall time.
● Chart it and match or beat when this session is repeated.
● Five seconds over on the repeat buys you two more 50s.

NSR 3. Suicide sprint & backpedal
● Perform as you would the standard Suicide Run but once you touch each line, backpedal to the start to work the anterior chain.
● Chart and use the same penalty protocol when repeated.

NSR 4. Bear start 10/40s
● Mark off a course as follows: 0 yards, 10 yards and 50 yards.
● 10/40s follow the same protocol each time with the only change being what is to be performed in the 10 yard stretch.

● On the whistle, bear crawl (crawl on hands and feet) as quickly as possible to the 10 yard line, burst to your feet and finish the remaining 40 yards as quickly as possible.
● Walk back to 0. If you've done it right, you'll appreciate the walk.
● Ten rounds score overall time and apply the five-second penalty rule.

NSR 5. 10/100s
● Ten 100-yard dashes with a strict 60 seconds of rest between efforts.
● Score overall time and observe the penalty rule.

NSR 6. Prisoner jump squat 10/40s
● Perform prisoner jump squats for 10 yards.
● At the 10-yard line, burst into your fastest 40-yard dash.
● Repeat 10 times.
● Chart and add penalties next time around.

By this point you get the charting and penalty process. By recording and benchmarking the workouts, you make a loose commitment to always strive for maximum effort. You shortchange yourself if you dial down the effort or remove the prospect of penalties.

NSR 7. Your fastest mile
● You guessed it — run it, chart it, match or beat it next time out or you get to add another half mile to your day.

NSR 8. 5 X 5
● Best performed on a demarcated track or field.
● Run all out for five minutes.
● Rest for three minutes.
● Perform for five rounds.
● Chart your maximum distance covered.
● Penalty is another five-minute round for every 50 yards you fall short of your previous performance.

NSR 9. Full suicides

● Perform the standard suicide run (NSR 1), but instead of finishing after touching the 50 yard line ...

● Work back down through 40, 30, 20 and 10.

● Rest three minutes and then hit one more round.

NSR 10. Hill sprints

● Work the steepest hills you can manage.

● Aim for hills that are at least 100 yards long with inclination along the entire path.

● Hit 10 hill sprints.

● Your rest is your walk down.

● Chart it and match or beat your time next time.

● Five seconds or more over, add two more hill sprints.

● If you lack hills in your area, add a weight vest, backpack loaded with a few plates or a drag bag and do a series of 100 yards.

NSR 11. Broad jump start 10/40s

● Perform standing broad jumps for maximum distance for the first 10 yards and then sprint the remaining 40.

● Walk back, repeat 10 times.

NSR 12. 5 X 3

● Use the same distance approach as you do in the 5 X 5, but here your time interval is three minutes on and one minute of rest.

● Five rounds total.

Once you've made it through this 12-part cycle, start over, or you can augment with additional workouts found at our Web site www.extremeselfprotection.com. Click on the inTENS section.

5.4 Double Dutch

Wanna skip rope? I mean rope skipping has a long tradition in boxing, right? It is used to condition both legs and stamina, but does it do the same job as sprinting? Nope, not even close. Yes, a skilled rope skipper can get the heart rate up there, but not anywhere near the threshold that can be reached via sprint work (or rapid metabolic lifting for that matter). With that in mind, you've got to decide for yourself if you are including rope skipping in your training out of fealty to tradition or are you simply avoiding harder, more efficient work?

I think you know where I sit on this topic, but if you still wanna skip, here's a little info. Here is another loose survey of the number of three-minute rounds champs put into their rope skipping per session.

1-2 rounds	0%
3-4 rounds	39%
5-6 rounds	58%
8-9 rounds	3%

If we look at the time eaten by the majority of rope skippers (58 percenters), there is approximately 18 minutes of training time taken up by a suboptimum leg and stamina builder. In the same time you could hit both an NS Roadwork Workout to build superior wind and leg stamina, rest three minutes and then run a few rounds of the Footwork Tango to work boxing specific footwork as opposed to rope skipping specific footwork.

If you choose to skip, skip fast!

Still wanna skip rope? OK, if you're going to do it, let's at least get maximum utility out of the effort.

Rule #1
Keep the rope turnover rate fast. Slow skipping means you might as well be walking.

Rule #2
One jump per turnover. If you've got time to add an extra jump between turnovers (pepper time) you're skipping too slowly.

Rule #3
Doubles, triples and quints (jumping high enough to allow for two, three or even four passes of the rope per jump) are the only "tricks" you really need. Sure you can skip side to side, cross your arms in front of your body, recite a cute rhyme if you'd like, but these are skills that add appreciably little to your boxing development. They're fun to do, they're neat to look at, but what exactly do they have to do with boxing? Nothing really. Rope tricks are sort of like speed bag work for your feet — neat but really of nominal practical utility.

With the aforementioned doubles, triples and quints, we finally bring rope skipping up to snuff as a stamina builder. But you'll not be able to maintain doubles, triples and quints for 5-6 rounds (probably not even one continuous round if you're honest with yourself).

With that info in mind, you can opt for Old School skipping choosing a target number of rounds from the Champions' Bell Curve or you can try New School skipping in one of two ways:

- Double, triple or quint for 20 seconds.
- Rest 10 seconds.
- Repeat this sequence eight times.

Or

- 50 doubles, triples or quints.
- Rest 30 seconds
- Repeat five times.

I give you no more New School skip routines than that because there's higher quality work that you could be doing.

5.5 Heavy bag

The heavy bag is one serious piece of training gear. You want to build boxing specific wind? Bang the bag. You want to build boxing specific power? Bang the bag. When you lack a training partner, the heavy bag is one high-yielding tool. It doesn't matter if you bang an Old School bag, an uppercut bag, a teardrop bag, or any other inventive variety on the market — as a boxer you've got to put some serious time into bag work.

How much time? Again, two choices. You can select a designated number of rounds from the Champions' Bell Curve or you can opt for some of the New School variations offered in the menus. First, though, the survey of champions' heavy bag rounds per training session is as follows:

3 rounds per session   3%
4 rounds per session   52%
6 rounds per session   45%

Before we get to New School approaches to the bag, a few words on how to approach the bag.

Rule #1
Bring your imagination to the bag. Don't bang mindlessly. The best champions actively envision a living, breathing, moving opponent in front of them. They keep good guard and strive to hit hard while leaving as few holes to be hit as possible. As useful as the heavy bag is, it is also a major contributor of bad habits since some athletes get lazy on the heavy bag. That is, they adopt atrocious defensive form in the pur-

suit of maximum bang. Don't be that guy. See that living, breathing opponent in front of you.

Rule #2
Let technique, not muscle reveal your power. A huge novice mistake is to bang for all you're worth, as hard as you can while giving no thought to how you hit. Good punching technique is based on body mechanics and timing, not strength or mass. Strength and mass are vital, yes, but they are meant to support good technique, not to be the primary drivers of good technique.

Rule #3
Snapping the bag is better than swinging the bag. The more the bag swings when you punch it, the more you're pushing your punches rather than snapping them. Pushing is a sign of poor technique (or fatigue). You want good technique to fire your punches with quick, snappy impacts.

Rule #4
Be a boxer not a Toughman competitor. To the boxer, a punch is a work of art, a precise tool to be delivered with maximum technique. The Toughman swings and wings it left and right. Many people assume that because they can form a fist and strike something, they are boxing — nothing could be further from the truth. Boxing is a precise and scientific skill set with specific form and technique. Banging the bag with spastic form no more makes you a boxer than throwing lazy spirals in the front yard makes you a quarterback.

Rule #5

Move. The stationary nature of the heavy bag leads some boxers (even some good intermediate fighters) to play the bag somewhat stock still. Let's remember, how you train is how you'll fight. Use footwork to get you inside and out on the bag. Move your head after you hit. Rough it with the shoulders inside the clinch and pop back out. The bag may be stationary, but you should never be.

Heavy bag SPP menus

All heavy bag SPP drills (and all remaining boxing SPP for that matter) require a three round minimum. You can always do more, but if you want progress you should never shoot for less.

Combination laddering
● Use any combination from the combination menu and build it as follows …
● Assuming we pick JAB HEAD / CROSS HEAD / LEAD HOOK HEAD
● JAB HEAD — Move
● JAB HEAD / CROSS HEAD — Move
● JAB HEAD / CROSS HEAD / LEAD HOOK HEAD — Move
● Repeat the ladder steps.

Footwork Tango two step
● Pick any two steps from the Footwork Tango.
● Pick any one combination from the Combination Menu.
● Ladder the combination while working the designated foot-work.
● Example: Quick Advance — JAB HEAD — Quick Advance — JAB HEAD / CROSS HEAD

Head hunter
● Emphasize working all forms of head shots.

Body killer
● Emphasize banging the body.

Outsider
● Throw all punches as if you had an 82-inch reach.

Insider
● Move that head, get inside and bang as if you had a reach of only 60 inches.

Match or beat: 30 seconds
● You can use match or beat to compete against a partner or your own time(s).
● Set a timer for the designated time.
● Bang the bag all out while your coach/partner keeps a punch count.
● Rest one minute.
● Repeat: You must match or beat the first punch count or perform 25 prisoner squats for every five punches under.
● Perform for three rounds.

Match or beat: one minute
● See the preceding drill.

Match or beat: two minutes
● Ditto.

Match or beat: 90 seconds

Match or beat: three minutes

Out-of-plumb sprints
● Get your head on the bag and lean in until the bag is out of plumb.
● On the go, you must use nothing but punches to keep the bag out of plumb for the designated time.
● This is grueling. I suggest a series of 30-60 second bursts for this one.

7 & 7: Outside / inside
● Have your coach/training partner keep a second stopwatch for this one.
● For the first seven seconds, bang the bag as an outside fighter. For the next seven seconds, bang it as an infighter.
● Alternate every seven seconds until the round is up.

7 & 7: Head / body

● Use the 7 & 7 protocol alternating head hunting and body killing.

7 & 7: Left / right

● Use the 7 & 7 protocol for punches all off the left hand and then all off the right hand.

Beat on the beat

● You can use a metronome or your favorite piece of music — the faster paced the better.
● Keep the beat with your fists.

Jazz

● Free form on the bag.
● I advise using Jazz about every third session. Keeping a goal or plan when you approach the bag is ideal because you are always working for a new skill or better times on drills. Jazz has a tendency to allow us to fall into pet form and grooves.

5.6 Shadowboxing & mirror work

Whether you use a mirror to check form or your imagination to conjure an opponent in front of you, "fighting air" is a long time staple of boxing training. Although it is not necessarily a physically grueling endeavor, it is vital when approached properly.

Shadowboxing and mirror work give you the freedom to work a marriage of scripted and free form (Jazz) footwork/punch combinations. Fighting air allows you to educate precise movement without the onus of having to prove something by loading up your punches. Fighting air allows you to educate punch recovery, that is the pull back or negative portion of the punch, which is important because you will miss way more than you hit in an actual match.

As usual, there are two ways to approach shadowboxing/mirror work — Old School and New School. Our Champions' Bell Curve breaks down the average rounds of shadowboxing per session as follows:

1 round per session	3%
2 rounds per session	0%
3 rounds per session	55%
4 rounds per session	23%
5 rounds per session	2%
6 rounds per session	17%

For the New School approach, let's ballpark in the majority choice, three three-minute rounds.

Shadowboxing SPP menus

Combination laddering
● Use any combination from the Combination Menu and build it as follows...
● Assuming we pick JAB HEAD / CROSS HEAD / LEAD HOOK HEAD
● JAB HEAD — Move
● JAB HEAD / CROSS HEAD — Move
● JAB HEAD / CROSS HEAD / LEAD HOOK HEAD — Move
● Repeat the ladder steps.

Footwork Tango two-step
● Pick any two steps from the Footwork Tango.
● Pick any one combination from the Combination Menu.
● Ladder the combination while working the designated footwork.
● Example: Quick Advance — JAB — Quick Advance — JAB / CROSS

Head hunter
● Emphasize working all forms of head shots.

Body killer
● Emphasize banging the body.

Outsider
● Throw all punches as if you had an 82-inch reach.

Insider
● Move that head, get inside and bang as if you had a reach of only 60 inches.

Beat on the beat
● You can use a metronome or your favorite piece of music —

the faster paced the better.
● Keep the beat with your fists.

Leftie
● Fight all three rounds with only left-hand punches.

Rightie
● You know what to do.

Mime in a box
● Mark a 36-inch square on the floor.
● Use as much head movement, bobbing and weaving, drop shifting as you can put together while confining yourself to this 36-inch square.

Road runner
● Stay on your toes and use the entire ring/training area as you stay mobile as possible.

Jazz
● Free form.
● I advise using Jazz only about every third session. Keeping a goal or plan when you approach the bag is ideal as you are always working for a new skill or better times on drills. Jazz has a tendency to allow us to fall into pet form and grooves.

Fighting air allows you to educate precise movement without the onus of having to prove something by loading up your punches.

5.7 Double-end bag

The double-end bag is a fun piece of gear that is akin to the speed bag, but it more closely resembles actual boxing than the both-hands-high, strike-with-the-hammer-fist technique of the speed bag. The double-end bag is used to build eye-hand coordination, upper body movement and punch rate. For these purposes it cannot touch focus pad work for utility, but it will do if a feeder is unavailable.

The double-end was used by very few of the champions in our survey (interestingly enough the speed bag was used even less, which seems to confirm our suspicions about its utility). The Champions' Bell Curve ballparks rounds devoted to the double-end as follows:

2 rounds per session   3%
3 rounds per session   95%
4 rounds per session   2%

For the New School approach, let's adopt the majority three rounds approach.

Double-end bag SPP menus

Combination laddering
● Use any combination from the Combination Menu and build it as follows …
● Assuming we pick JAB HEAD / CROSS HEAD / LEAD HOOK HEAD
● JAB HEAD — Move
● JAB HEAD / CROSS HEAD — Move
● JAB HEAD / CROSS HEAD / LEAD HOOK HEAD — Move
● Repeat the ladder steps.

Bobby weaver
● Fire a big shot and get tight to the bag attempting to use head and body movement to not be touched on any rebound.

Outsider
● Throw all punches as if you had an 82-inch reach.

Insider
● Move that head, get inside and bang as if you had a reach of only 60 inches

Match or beat: 30 seconds
● You can use match or beat to compete against a partner or your own time(s).
● Set a timer for the designated time.
● Bang the bag all out while your coach/partner keeps a punch count—only count punches that contact the bag.
● Rest one minute.
● Repeat: You must match or beat the first punch count or perform 25 prisoner squats for every five punches under.
● Perform for three rounds.

Match or beat: one minute
● See the preceding drill.

Match or beat: two minutes
● Ditto.

Match or beat: 90 seconds

Match or beat: three minutes

7 & 7: Left / right
● Use the 7 & 7 protocol for punches all with the left hand and then all with the right hand.

Leftie
● Fight all three rounds with only left-hand punches.

Rightie
● You know what to do.

Beat on the beat
● You can use a metronome or your favorite piece of music—the faster paced the better.
● Keep the beat with your fists.

Jazz
● Free form on the bag.
● I advise using Jazz about every third session. Keeping a goal or plan when you approach the bag is ideal as you are always working for a new skill or better times on drills. Jazz has a tendency to allow us to fall into pet form and grooves.

5.8 Rope weaving

Good boxers have excellent head movement. They move their head before a punch, after a punch, even when not punching. Nothing will build superior head and upper body movement like a good focus pad feeder or focused sparring. But a standard line of rope will serve in a pinch for solo sessions.

Any rope/cord/string will do if you can span it at least 10 feet in your training area. Tie the rope off at shoulder height so that you have a realistic height to work with. Tying too low, while a good leg conditioner, teaches exaggerated movement, and good boxing is about economy of motion. Being missed by inches is as good as being missed by a mile and is far less tiring.

This training method popped up in the regimens of only five champions — it was a big favorite of the crafty Aaron Pryor. But if you are going to incorporate it, let's go with our industry standard of three three-minute rounds.

Rope weaving SPP menus

Static bob & weave
● Take a stance to one side of the rope — here to the left of the rope.
● Bob and weave to come up on the right side of the rope.
● Repeat to the left.

Static bob & weave hooks
● Perform the bob & weave, but as you come up on each side fire a hook.

Static bob & weave uppercuts
● You know what to do.

Bob & weave walk
● Start at one end of the rope and travel the length of the rope taking one step per bob and weave.

Bob & weave walk hooks
● Combine the weave walk with throwing hooks on the upswing of each bob.

Bob & weave walk uppercuts
● You know what to do.

Retreating bob & weave walk
● Yep, now try it moving backward.

Retreating bob & weave walk hooks

Retreating bob & weave walk uppercuts

Rope weaving jazz
● Improvise, my friends.

Champion's tale #8

Double trouble

Dmitri Salita has occasionally used two sparring partners simultaneously to keep him on the move.

Feeding actively means pushing the pace and hitting back.

5.9 Focus pads

We now move to a piece of gear that you can't play solo — focus pads or punch mitts. Focus pads are formidable skill builders, but only if your feeder (focus pad holder) brings something to the table. Simply slipping your hands into some mitts and holding them up for some variety of punches is a waste of everyone's time. The lazy feeder could be off somewhere reading a magazine instead, and the boxer would be better off working any of the aforementioned pieces of gear with scientific intent. With this in mind, I offer the following feeder's guidelines ...

Feeder's guidelines

1. It's a 50/50 partnership. You, the feeder, are just as vital as the boxer. What you bring to the drill is equal to what the boxer will get out of it. A lazy feeder will create an untaxed boxer. A sloppy feeder will create a sloppy boxer. And an active, focused feeder will create a crafty boxer.

2. Be a boxer. The best feeders become living, active opponents in front of their boxer. They move, they push the pace, they hit back and feeders get to do all of this without the pain of getting hit back. Sweet, huh?

3. Hold the pads near their corresponding targets. Feeding a head shot? Hold that pad as comfortably near your head as you can manage. Feeding the body? Get those pads near your body, not held out at arm's length away from you. Don't force your boxer to punch unreasonably wide. Let them see the human body as a target, not a scarecrow with targets always extended at arm's length.

4. *Hit back part one.* Don't just let your hands be smacked. Smack back a little into those punches so that your boxer feels some resistance. The smack back need not be exaggerated. No need to meet your boxer halfway and reduce his work. Smack back enough to give him something to bite, but don't move toward his punches creating a pugilistic form of patty-cake.

5. *Hit back part two.* Did your boxer swim his jab leaving his chin open? Hit that hole. Did he fail to move his head after certain combinations? Hit that head. If you don't hit your boxer, you are nothing more than a glorified heavy bag and guess what — that job is already taken. Hit your boxer back. That's why you put the mitts on.

Focus pad SPP menus

The feeder should always fire back looking for holes in every version of these drills.

Combination laddering
● Use any combination from the Combination Menu and build it as follows …
● Assuming we pick JAB HEAD / CROSS HEAD / LEAD HOOK HEAD
● JAB HEAD — Move
● JAB HEAD / CROSS HEAD — Move
● JAB HEAD / CROSS HEAD / LEAD HOOK HEAD — Move
● Repeat the ladder steps.

Footwork Tango two-step
● The best version of this drill as a good feeder can lead you into some interesting footwork scenarios.
● Pick any two steps from the Footwork Tango.
● Pick any one combination from the Combination Menu.
● Ladder the combination while working the designated footwork.
● Example: Quick advance — JAB HEAD — Quick advance — JAB HEAD / CROSS HEAD

Head hunter
● Emphasize working all forms of head shots.

Body killer
● Emphasize banging the body.

Outsider
● Throw all punches as if you had an 82-inch reach.
● The feeder should constantly push trying to kill the reach.

Insider

● Move that head, get inside and bang as if you had a reach of only 60 inches.
● The top level of this drill has the feeder firing shots that the boxer must move inside of before banging.

Leftie

● Fight all three rounds with only left-hand punches.

Rightie

● You know what to do.

Mime in a box

● Mark a 36-inch square on the floor.
● Use as much head movement, bobbing and weaving, drop shifting as you can put together while confining yourself to this 36-inch square.

Road runner

● Stay on your toes and use the entire ring/training area as you stay mobile as possible.

Jazz

● Here the boxer is reacting to the feeder's jazz improvisations.
● I advise using jazz about every third session. Keeping a goal or plan when you approach the bag is ideal as you are always working for a new skill or better times on drills. Jazz has a tendency to allow us to fall into pet form and grooves.

Rhythm feeding

● These drills are used to condition your boxer's shoulders. Pick one of the patterns from the rhythm feeding menu, and your boxer will attempt to hold to a constant pace with continuous punching and very little gaps/pauses in firing (fatigue will definitely be a factor).

● Here there is no need for the feeder to fire at the holes, just keep the pace up for the boxer.

● Think of this as speed bag work with better form.

● Example of rhythm feeding: the rhythm feed RLRR LRLL

● R = Right-handed punches

● L = Left-handed punches

● The boxer must fire a right, left, right-right to left, right, left-left combination and then immediately restart the pattern.

● The goal is maximum speed with zero lag in pace.

More rhythm feeds
● RRRR LLLL
● RRLL RRLL
● RLLR LRRL
● RRLR LLRL
● RLRR LLRL
● RLRR LRRL
● RRLR LRLL
● RRLR LRRL
● RLLR LRLL
● RLLR LLRL

As you can see the variations are numerous and are easily improvised.

Sidebar
Focus pads also lend themselves quite well to working flow drills, which are long offensive/defensive combination chains. We'll get back to this idea after exploring the place that sparring has in your training.

... the goal of sparring is not to "beat" your partner, but to emphasize the targeted skill and make it manifest itself under pressure.

5.10 Sparring

Two things up front that usually surprise boxing rookies …

#1: Sparring is not fighting. Sparring is not a match. Sparring resembles an actual bout in many respects, but it is a way to train specific tactics and strategies in a limited "fight" context. Yes, you can (and will) be hit just as in an actual bout, but the goal of sparring is not to "beat" your partner, but to emphasize the targeted skill and make it manifest itself under pressure.

#2: Champs spar far less than you might think. In our Champions' Bell Curve, champs hit the heavy bag a lot, worked shadowboxing for mucho rounds and worked focus pads hard, hard, hard. But a remarkably light 23 percent made sparring a regular part of their training regimen.

Why might this be? One, they are already champs and they already know how to box. But the more likely answer is that they do not want to risk injury before the actual bout.

Those who did/do make targeted sparring a part of their training emphasized sparring in the beginning of their training camp and tapered off as the actual fight date approached. This seems to confirm the "protect against injuries" hypothesis.

When sparring was included, it is almost an even split between those who hit four rounds per session and those who hit six rounds per session.

Again, the number of champs who used sparring is/was light. The vast majority did little to no sparring in preparation for a bout.

Those of us still on the path to 10,000 hours don't have the luxury to shirk this work, but we can learn something about where priorities lie in the brains of the best champions and trainers. And keep in mind, those who did/do include sparring always used it in a targeted fashion. That is, to work specific ideas — not to make the sparring session just an informal bout.

Sparring SPP menus

Combination laddering
● In this version, both boxers are laddering in a tit for tat fashion, but the goal is to make contact and to make your partner miss.

Footwork Tango two-step
● Again, both fighters have the two-step and ladder in mind.
● Your job is to make contact and make your partner miss.
● Pick any two-steps from the Footwork Tango.
● Pick any one combination from the combination menu.
● Ladder the combination while working the designated footwork.

One for one
● Boxer A throws any single shot.
● Boxer B defends (or eats it) and returns his single shot.
● Continue.

Two for two
● You know what to do.

Three for three
● Ditto.

One for two
● Boxer A gets one shot, Boxer B gets two shots.
● Switch roles the next round.

One for three
● Are we sensing a pattern here?

Two for three
● Yeah, that's a pattern.

Isolation sparring
Here, both fighters assume the same roles (that is, head hunter vs. head hunter) or you can mix and match (say, insider vs. rightie).

Head hunter
● Emphasize working all forms of head shots.

Body killer
● Emphasize banging the body.

Outsider
● Throw all punches as if you had an 82-inch reach.

Insider
● Move that head, get inside and bang as if you had a reach of only 60 inches.

Leftie
● Fight all three rounds with only left-hand punches.

Rightie
● You know what to do.

Cornered
● One boxer must stay in the corner and fight from there.
● Use as much head movement, bobbing and weaving, drop shifting as you can put together while confining yourself to the corner.

On the ropes & off

● One boxer starts with his back to the ropes and must fight from there unless or until the coach commands him to move off the ropes.

● The other boxer's job is to keep his man on the ropes.

The general

● You must command the center of the ring at all costs.

Road runner

● Stay on your toes and use the entire ring/training area while you remain mobile as possible.

Jazz

● Use seldom as this can quickly turn into a bout and/or allow you to fall back into complacency (pet moves).

● Treat it as an actual bout but control for contact.

5.11 Flow drills for focus pads & sparring

Flow drills allow two active participants to work pre-arranged offensive/defensive combination patterns. From the outside, when worked up to speed, flow drills resemble brief flurries of an actual bout, and that is a mighty good thing. Flow drills allow the boxer to hone specific tactics and strategies up to speed while conditioning "ring feel." That is, how it feels to be in the thick of things.

Flow drills are complex skill work and can number into the stratosphere. Here, we introduce just a few flow drills to get you started on the concept and save cataloging the 100-plus flow drills and trigger boxing concepts (trigger boxing is drilling for reflexive counterpunching) for another day. You're not being short-changed. Once you get these example patterns under your belt, you can use the companion manual, *Boxing Mastery*, and with a little ingenuity, create your own flows.

Flow drills notation

Boxer A, or simply A, is the initiating boxer (or focus pad feeder). His actions are described outside of parentheses.

Boxer B, or B, is the responder. His actions are described inside parentheses.

Flow drill protocol

● Work each link in a flow drill chain for one three-minute round.

● If it feels right and grooves, add the next link. Always begin with link one and add the subsequent links.

● If at any point there is a link that's a little iffy, don't move beyond that link until it's down pat.

● Again, always start at link one and move forward adding links as you go. Do not work them in isolation.

● Boxers A and B keep the same roles throughout.

● Once a chain has been mastered, reverse the roles as each individual chain is two drills in one.

Sample flow drill SPP menus

Check out the three drills illustrated on the next three pages. As you can see, these drills can be multiplied ad naseum and can be tailored to specific tactical needs. To create your own, consult our book, *Boxing Mastery*, or visit our Web site www.extremeselfprotection.com where we provide additional flow chain resources.

Jab head (catch) · *+ Cross head (block)* · *+ (Cross head)* · *+ (Lead hook body)* · *+ (Lead hook head)*

Flow drill #1

1. Jab (catch)
2. + Cross (block)
3-5. + (Cross/lead hook body/lead hook head)

Jab (catch) | + Rear hook (bob & weave)

+ (Lead shovel hook body) | + (Lead hook head)

Flow drill #2

1. Jab (catch)
2. + Rear hook (bob & weave)
3. + (Lead shovel hook body)
4. + (Lead hook head)

Jab (catch)   + Cross (block)

+ Hook (duck)   + (Cross head)

+ (Lead uppercut)   + (Cross head)

+ (Lead hook head)

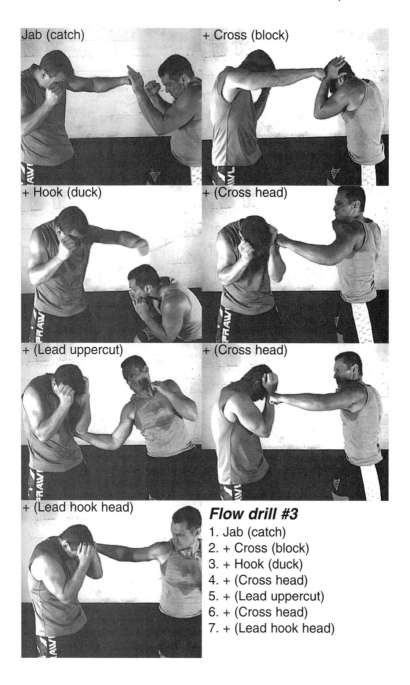

Flow drill #3

1. Jab (catch)
2. + Cross (block)
3. + Hook (duck)
4. + (Cross head)
5. + (Lead uppercut)
6. + (Cross head)
7. + (Lead hook head)

The End?

The end of this book, yes, but not the end of your journey to 10,000 hours of accumulated mastery. I wish you all the best on your journey, and as already mentioned, we provide additional resources to augment your training and material specific to this book at our Web site.

Train harder, train smarter, and have fun while you do it!

Mark Hatmaker
www.extremeselfprotection.com

Resources

BEST CHOICES

First, please visit my Web site at
www.extremeselfprotection.com
You will find even more training
material as well as updates and
other resources.

Amazon.com

The place to browse for books such
as this one and other similar titles.

Paladin Press
www.paladin-press.com

Paladin carries many training
resources as well as some of my
videos, which allow you to see
much of what is covered in my
NHB books.

Ringside Boxing
www.ringside.com

Best choice for primo equipment.

Sherdog.com

Best resource for MMA news, event
results and NHB happenings.

Threat Response Solutions
www.trsdirect.com

They also offer many training
resources along with some of my
products.

Tracks Publishing
www.trackspublishing.com

They publish all the books in the
NHBF series and MMA series as
well as a few fine boxing titles.

www.humankinetics.com

Training and conditioning info.

www.matsmatsmats.com

Best resource for quality mats at
good prices.

Video instruction

Extreme Self-Protection
extremeselfprotection.com

Paladin Press
paladin-press.com

Threat Response Solutions
trsdirect.com

World Martial Arts
groundfighter.com

Events

IFC
ifc-usa.com

IVC
valetudo.com

King of the Cage
kingofthecage.com

Pancrase
so-net.ne.jp/pancrase

Pride
pridefc.com

The Ultimate Fighting
Championships
ufc.tv

Universal Combat Challenge
ucczone.ca/

Index

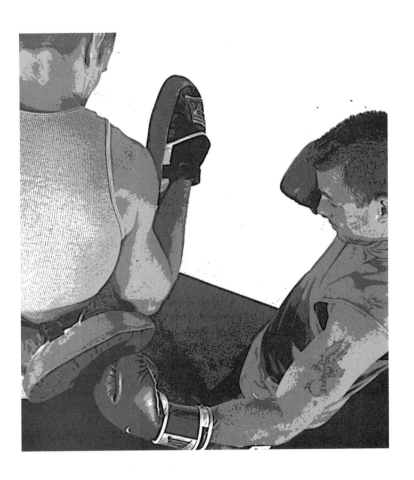

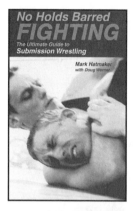
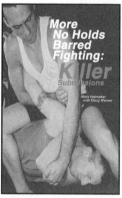
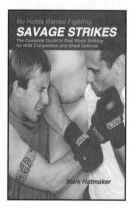

Boxing Mastery
*Advance Techniques, Tactics and
Strategies from the Sweet Science*
Advanced boxing skills and ring general-
ship.
978-1-884654-29-9 / $12.95
900 photos

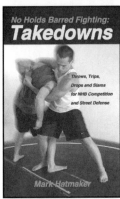

**No Holds Barred Fighting:
Takedowns**
*Throws, Trips, Drops and Slams for NHB
Competition and Street Defense*
978-1-884654-25-1 / $12.95
850 photos

**No Holds Barred Fighting:
The Clinch**
*Offensive and Defensive Concepts
Inside NHB's Most Grueling Position*
978-1-884654-27-5 / $12.95
750 photos

No Holds Barred Fighting:
The Ultimate Guide to Conditioning
Elite Exercises and Training for NHB
Competition and Total Fitness
978-1-884654-29-9 / $12.95
900 photos

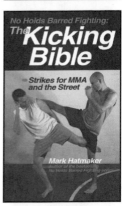

No Holds Barred Fighting:
The Kicking Bible
Strikes for MMA and the Street
978-1-884654-31-2 / $12.95
700 photos

No Second Chance:
A Reality-Based Guide to Self-Defense
How to avoid and survive an assault.
978-1-884654-32-9 / $12.95
500 photos

No Holds Barred Fighting:
The Book of Essential Submissions
How MMA champions gain their victories. A catalog of winning submissions.
978-1-884654-33-6 / $12.95
750 photos

MMA Mastery: Flow Chain Drilling
and Integrated O/D Training
to Submission Wrestling
Blends all aspects of the MMA fight game into devastating performances.
978-1-884654-38-1 / $13.95
800 photos

MMA Mastery: Ground and Pound
A comprehensive go-to guide — how to win on the ground.
978-1-884654-39-8 / $13.95
650 photos

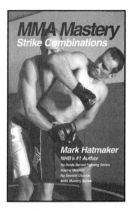

MMA Mastery: Strike Combinations
Learn the savage efficiency of striking in combinations. A comprehensive guide.
978-1-935937-22-7 / $12.95
1000 photos

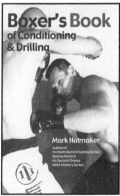

Boxer's Book of Conditioning & Drilling
How to get fighting fit like the champions.
978-1-935937-28-9 / $12.95
650 photos

Mark Hatmaker is the bestselling author of the *No Holds Barred Fighting Series,* the *MMA Mastery Series, No Second Chance* and *Boxing Mastery.* He also has produced more than 40 instructional

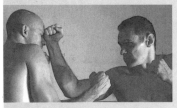 videos. His resume includes extensive experience in the combat arts including boxing, wrestling, Jiu-jitsu and Muay Thai.

He is a highly regarded coach of professional and amateur fighters, law enforcement officials and security personnel. Hatmaker founded Extreme Self Protection (ESP), a research body that compiles, analyzes and teaches the most effective Western combat methods known. ESP holds numerous seminars throughout the country each year including the prestigious Karate College/Martial Arts Universities in Radford, Virginia. He lives in Knoxville, Tennessee.

 www.extremeselfprotection.com
